Children
And
Residential
Experiences

Creating Conditions for Change

Children And Residential Experiences

Edition 2

Creating Conditions for Change

Written by

Martha J. Holden MS

With the following faculty of the Residential Child Care Project

Tom Endres MA
Joanna F. Garbarino BS
John Gibson MSW, MSSc, CQSW
Jack C. Holden PhD
I. Franklin Kuhn, Jr. PhD
Carla Morgan MEd
Michael A. Nunno DSW
Mary Ruberti MSW
Angela Stanton-Greenwood MA, MEd

2009, Residential Child Care Project, Cornell University

CWLA Press is an imprint of CWLA. CWLA is the nation's oldest and largest membership-based child welfare organization. We are committed to engaging people everywhere in promoting the well-being of children, youth, and their families, and protecting every child from harm. All proceeds from the sale of this book support CWLA's programs in behalf of children and families.

© 2009 Residential Child Care Project, Cornell University
Family Life Development Center, Beebe Hall, Ithaca, NY 14853
http://rccp.cornell.edu

Published by
The Child Welfare League of America
1726 M St. NW, Suite 500
Washington, DC 20036
www.cwla.org

CURRENT PRINTING (last digit)
10 9 8 7 6 5 4 3

Cover and text design by Wells Communications, Ithaca, New York

ISBN: 978-1-58760-126-2

Holden, Martha J.
  Children and residential experiences : creating conditions for change / written by Martha J. Holden. -- Ed. 2.
       p. cm.
  Includes bibliographical references and index.
  ISBN 978-1-58760-126-2 (pbk. : alk. paper)
  1. Children--Institutional care--United States. 2. Group homes for children--United States. 3. Social work with children--United States. I. Residential Child Care Project. II. Child Welfare League of America. III. Title.
  HV863.H65 2009
  362.73'20973--dc22

                                                      2009050320

This book is dedicated to children living in out-of-home care and the devoted professionals who care for them.

Contents

Foreword

Welcome to the CARE program model. The CARE program model represents a new approach and a new generation of training for residential child and youth care work. The Residential Child Care Project at Cornell University has long been a leader in child and youth care training, and in this new curriculum, the Project has brought together in a unified manner the best practices derived from the work and wisdom of the field's top practitioners with the latest knowledge and frameworks derived from residential care research.

Initial feedback from agencies utilizing this approach indicates that it is both challenging and liberating. It is challenging because it places prime importance on the practitioner's ability to be self-aware, reflective, and truly responsive—not just reactive. It is liberating as it frees the worker to help to heal the pain and trauma at the heart of young peoples' experiences, rather than directing them to focus on controlling behavior.

The sub-title of this text, "creating the conditions for change," emphasizes both the need for enhancing young people's development and the fact that young people are always "in charge" of their own behavior. Our job as child and youth care practitioners in residential care is to create an environment conducive to growth and to respond therapeutically to the situations and struggles of the residents and their families.

But make no mistake—this is tough work that requires rigorous training and ongoing supervision of the highest order; thus the need for a powerful, integrated and well-grounded model for understanding and addressing residential life and residential child and youth care practice. But the lives of the young people, and their futures, are worth the struggle and they deserve our very best efforts.

Finally, research has demonstrated that effective residential care practice requires the commitment and active participation of the entire residential agency and system. It must be a system that is congruent with the responsive carework needed by the young people themselves. At each level of the organization, and across all levels of the system, the core principles and effective interactional dynamics that comprise the foundation of this approach need to be modeled and practiced. Any agency taking on a commitment to implement this CARE program model is to be applauded and encouraged.

I am confident that this book will prove to be a rich resource for managers, trainers, and workers alike, and that the quality of residential care in agencies utilizing this material in a conscious and disciplined way will be significantly enhanced.

Jim Anglin PhD
Professor, School of Child and Youth Care
University of Victoria, BC, Canada

In Memoriam

There is a special place in our hearts for Nancy K. Perry, former Executive Director of the South Carolina Association of Children's Homes and Family Services. Nancy's visionary leadership and compassion for children and families gave this project life, and it was through her efforts that the CARE program exists. The basic principles contained in this book mirror her lifelong commitment to supporting agencies and their staff members who struggle to achieve congruence in the best interests of children and families. Nancy passed away in 2007.

Acknowledgements

Any project of this magnitude has benefitted from the support, leadership, and participation of many individuals and organizations over many years. The Residential Child Care Project has worked with hundreds of organizations and thousands of professional caregivers over the past 30 years and we extend a heartfelt thanks to all of them. Through these experiences, we have learned about providing positive experiences and quality care for children in out-of-home care.

The Residential Child Care Project has had and continues to have the opportunity to collaborate with professionals around the globe. This cadre of talented individuals who comprise the faculty of the RCCP, share their expertise and contribute to our many projects. With their advice, hard work, and investment, the RCCP is able to contribute to the field in many ways in addition to the CARE program.

Jim Anglin, Director of International Affairs and Adviser to the Provost and Professor at the School of Child and Youth Care at the University of Victoria, BC, Canada, was and continues to be a major influence in the development of the CARE program. Jim's research and writings, especially *Pain, Normality and the Struggle for Congruence: Reinterpreting Residential Care of Children and Youth* (Anglin, 2002), inspired and provided the underpinning of the CARE practice model. His personal participation throughout this project provided insight and support that was always welcomed and often needed.

We want to acknowledge and give heartfelt thanks to the children and staff members of the organizations that participated in this project. The staff members' enthusiasm, commitment, professionalism, and dedication to serving the best interests of the children informed and enriched this program. The children's responsiveness and candor kept us on course and true to our mission.

Contributing Agencies

Collins Home and Family Ministries, Seneca, SC, founded in 1979 to provide a home for needy children in South Carolina.

Miracle Hill Ministries Inc., Greenville, SC, provides a shelter program for at-risk teenage boys, a children's home with crisis long-term care and foster care for children from birth to 18.

New Foundations Children and Family Services Inc., Anderson, SC, specializes in caring for emotionally troubled children, adolescents, and families.

Tamassee DAR School, Tamassee, SC, provides a residential care program for school-aged children and a day-care program available to community residents.

York Place, York, SC, provides treatment to children and adolescents with significant psychiatric illness and impairment in behavioral, cognitive, emotional, physical, familial, and social functioning, and in need of intensive treatment in and out of home placement.

Epworth Children's Home, Columbia, SC, a place for children ages 4 to 18 to grow, learn, and be loved.

Connie Maxwell Children's Home, Greenwood, SC, provides hope for children and families dealing with difficult situations in their lives.

Generations Group Homes Inc., Simpsonville, SC, provides boys with a therapeutic environment that promotes and rewards positive change.

Carolina Youth Development Center, Charleston, SC, provides emergency shelter, residential treatment, day treatment, and preparation for independent living.

Billie Hardee Home for Boys, Darlington, SC, offers a variety of out-patient and residential treatment programs to accommodate the needs of at-risk teenage boys.

Hillside Family of Agencies, Varick Campus, NY, addresses the varied, diverse, and complex needs of children and families in crisis situations.

Without the initial encouragement and financial support of the following agencies, the CARE project would not exist today. Through their advocacy for vulnerable children and their willingness to provide financial support to projects that hope to serve the best interests of these children, the quality of residential services to children in South Carolina are continuously improved.

The South Carolina Association of Children's Homes and Family Services

The Duke Endowment

The South Carolina Department of Social Services

BUILDING A FOUNDATION

CHAPTER 1

Introduction: A Framework for Creating Change

What do we know about providing good residential care for children and what do we actually do? There is no shortage of theory, good quality empirical research, published reflective practice, or useful conceptual frameworks (Gibson, 2005). In fact, our knowledge far exceeds our practices (Belknap, 2001; Eisikovits & Beker, 1991; Gibson, 2003) and although much has changed in child care over the last 70 years, the gap between what we know and what we do with the knowledge seems as wide as ever. Why is there such a gap? There are factors at every level of the group care system that contribute to the lack of evidence-based practice and full utilization of what we already know.

At the state and policy level, group care is often considered an undesirable option and used only when nothing else is available to the child. When group care is viewed as *the last resort*, placements in residential care are often seen as an act of desperation (no one else will take the child), not a thoughtful, planned process based on an assessment of the needs of the child and the family and the resources of the organization. To further complicate the situation, funding of group care is often based on formulas that do not consider strong staff development and enrichment activities as essential elements of good residential care. When residential care is not valued or is considered an undesirable option, it will likely be misused and under funded, resulting in poor outcomes for children. When the contracting, funding, and placing agencies work in tandem with the residential organization to determine what services, standards, resources, and procedures will be in the best interests of the children, the stage is set for quality care and treatment for children who need a higher level of care and treatment.

At the management and administrative level of residential care, the struggle is often just to keep beds full and staffing ratios adequate to meet budgetary and licensing requirements. When faced with competing interests and priorities, decisions are not always made with the best interests of the children in mind or with the kind of consistency that communicates the value-base and overall vision of the organization (Anglin, 2002). To provide good quality services, the framework for care must be explicit and reinforced throughout the organization. The leaders must consistently share and act on the vision and values of the organization (Schein, 2004). When the leadership provides an underlying structure or framework for practice, staff and children can stay focused on their primary function and goals regardless of the changes and pressures placed upon the organization. Otherwise, other priorities, such as cost containment, staff preferences, and maintaining control, may be the force driving day-to-day decision-making and interactions between children and staff (Anglin, 2002).

At the supervisory level, expectations for practice are set and reinforced. Front line supervisors have the greatest impact on what skills and actions care workers will use on the job with the children (Curry, 1991). The supervisor's philosophy about how children are cared for will strongly influence the manner in which expectations for practice are set and reinforced, how members interact and support one another, and the way care workers treat the children. "Being supportively challenging" (Anglin, 2002, p. 92) by maintaining a balance between raising questions as to the effectiveness of staff actions and supporting staff in their pursuit of professional development, is an essential role of the supervisor.

If there is congruence between management and supervisors, it most likely will have a cascading effect and permeate the organization (Anglin, 2002). With the high rate of turnover and low priority on staff development, many supervisors are ill-prepared for communicating and mentoring an evidence-based framework for practice. Organizations that train and mentor supervisors to communicate professional expectations and work collaboratively with staff can sustain quality residential care that serves the best interests of the child.

Finally, at the care worker level, the framework for care provides care workers with clear objectives for daily routines, leisure activities, and staff-client interactions. This allows the care worker to focus on helping the children achieve the competencies necessary to manage life events successfully. Without a clear framework for providing care, there are lost opportunities throughout the day to use routines, staff-child interactions, and recreational activities to help clients achieve developmental and treatment goals. Care workers interact with young people based on their own interpretation of their role, the mission of the organization, the organizational climate and culture surrounding them, and their personal philosophy of child rearing. A framework for practice based on a valid theory of how children change, grow, and develop that is consistent with the needs of the children, motivates both children and staff to adhere to routines, structures, and processes and minimizes the potential for interpersonal conflict. A framework for practice provides consistency in message and approach with the children and congruency throughout the organization.

The overriding framework or core concept that drives good practice is "the struggle for congruence in the service for the best interests of the child" (Anglin, 2002, p. 52). This struggle for congruence encompasses three major properties: (1) Consistency in purpose, values, principles, and actions; (2) reciprocity demonstrated in the interactions between persons within the organization; and (3) cohesiveness or wholeness within the system of care. The concept of *the best interests of the child* is widely accepted as a touchstone for child and youth care practice and is reflected in the United Nations Convention on the Rights of the Child and in child welfare and child protection literature in North America and the United Kingdom. United in purpose, a well-functioning team/organization will struggle to achieve congruence in the best interests of the child when having to make difficult decisions that involve balancing competing needs, such as personal, organizational, and governmental requirements.

CHAPTER 2

Origins of Group Care

History is who we are and why we are the way we are.
—David C. McCullough

What We Know and When We Knew It

Adults have the responsibility of caring for children. When parents are unable or unavailable to fulfill this duty, other responsible adults step in to care for the child. Children being cared for by extended family and community is a practice that has a long history in many societies. The Circle of Courage or Caring (Brendtro, Brokenleg & Van Bockern, 1998) describes the care of children provided by tribes and villages in North America for thousands of years. Prior to the 17th century, Ireland was governed by a system of laws known as Brehon Laws (Robins, 1987). During this period, the tribe or clan took responsibility for the care of destitute, orphaned, or abandoned children. The child was cared for by the tribe and that child contributed to and strengthened the tribe.

Community responsibility for raising children is not a recent phenomenon, but has been around in many forms for centuries. It was generally recognized that this benefited both the child and the community.

Early Group Care: A Solution to Social Problems

In England, the Elizabethan Law of 1601 was the first law to assign public responsibility for needy children by placing them in almshouses (an early form of group care) and indenturing them to master craftsmen (an early form of foster care). The law was passed at the demand of the middle classes who wanted something done "to control the dangerous poor classes" and established these workhouses or almshouses for the orphans and the children of adults who worked under enforced conditions in other workhouses.

In ancient Ireland, children were cared for in monasteries by monks, but at the request of the citizens of Dublin who were concerned about vast numbers of vagrant children and beggars on the street, childcare became a public responsibility. In 1703, the first workhouse was opened and became the "national repository" for unwanted children (Robins, 1987). Other workhouses were established throughout the century to protect the citizens from encountering begging children on the street.

In North America during this period, orphanages, apprenticeships, reform schools, almshouses, and informal kinship care were the main components of a loose system of out-of-home care for most of the first two centuries of American history. Unfortunately, public need took priority over the needs of the children. *Institutionalized care* became synonymous with disadvantaged and destitute children, and impersonal, large institutions run by strict disciplinarians trying to maintain order and survive on donations and scant public funding: an image that lingers on even today.

The Industrial Age

The 18th and 19th centuries witnessed a change in the western world and a greater need for institutional care. With the increased urbanization came big city problems: long working hours, crime, unhealthy living conditions, poverty, and relaxed morals. Countries created prisons and insane asylums to deal with these social problems and sought ways to institutionalize the overpopulation of children on the streets. Orphanages provided an immediate solution to the bothersome problem of parentless children and a resolution to these social problems. The number of orphanages grew throughout the first half of the 19th Century largely in connection with epidemics, wars and conflicts, and an outpouring of religious benevolence. In addition to orphanages, adult jails were also used to *treat* delinquent children.

In the Best Interests of the Child

Toward the end of the 19th Century, both Catholic and Protestant churches were active in the provision of education and residential care in Ireland. In England, two significant proponents of philanthropic social work were Thomas Stephenson, founder of the National Children's Homes, and Thomas Barnardo, founder of the Dr. Barnardo's charity. The original mission of Barnardo's was to secure domestic work for the girls and to provide boys with a trade.

Additional pioneering individuals challenged "penal and punitive" (Balbernie, 1972) approaches to the care of children. As the 19th Century progressed, public concern about the plight of children in adult gaols (jails) found focus on both sides of the Irish Sea (Balbernie, 1972; Robins, 1987).

Mary Carpenter, a social reformer from Bristol, England, took note of humane developments in the treatment of delinquent children on the European Continent and argued for "humane and enlightened treatment of delinquent and homeless children." Carpenter also proposed a plan for reformatory schools for juvenile offenders and industrial schools for destitute children.

The Importance of Family

When orphanages became overcrowded in New York City, children were given train tickets and sent to the mid-western United States so that farm families could adopt them. This practice was discontinued during the 1930s when the Depression made it difficult for families to support additional children and new programs were being developed to provide foster care and help for children in their homes and communities.

In 1918, after the first World War, Barnardos began the practice of child migration to Australia and Canada. It was thought that these children needed a fresh start in the land of opportunity and that child migration could meet their needs.

This child migration remained unchallenged until after the second World War when children were evacuated to the countryside to save them from aerial bombing. The disruption of the war improved society's understanding of family break-up, loss, separation, and the effect on children of being brought up away from home. Anna Freud and Dorothy Burlingham provided a safe residential setting for young children who were from central London and in danger of bombings (Cohler & Zimmerman, 2000). Their reports of the children's emotional and behavioral problems as a result of separation from parents, moving to group care, reuniting with parents, and exposure to violence had a big impact on group care.

Trauma and Meeting Emotional Needs

In 1925, the first description of residential childcare organized explicitly on psychoanalytic lines appeared in the book *Wayward Youth* by August Aichorn (1925). Barbara Dockar-Drysdale (Dockar-Drysdale, 1968) began her work with children during World War II. She pioneered therapeutic work with children who experienced very early emotional deprivation. Janusz Korczak, a pediatrician who became the director of The House of Children in Warsaw, Poland in 1911, wrote 20 books about children (Wolins, 1967). Korczak concluded, "Your authority as a childcare worker is based on the strength of your status as a beloved and admired model person. This cannot be acquired by tools and technology" (Brendtro, 1990, p. 82).

These early pioneers established the importance of building relationships and paying attention to the emotional needs of children. Larry Brendtro (1990) identified themes promoted by pioneers that underpin best practice in residential care today: relationship and competence.

Relationships

August Aichorn in the early part of the 20th Century saw the relationship as the cornerstone of the re-education process. His ethic was that love must be dispensed to aggressive youth since it meets their unmet need. Alan Keith-Lucas, who came to the United States from England, saw love, acceptance, and understanding as the key to promoting positive behaviors. "One doesn't have to behave in order to be loved, but to be loved in order to behave" (Brendtro, 1990, p. 80). Al Trieschman, founder of the Walker School in Massachusetts, often spoke of his concern of professionalism overshadowing attachment. While visiting a group care facility, he declared that the social workers should place the children in the file cabinets where they would get more attention. He then added that the most important milestone for a youth worker was when the worker becomes a glimmer in the child's eye and the child becomes a glimmer in the worker's eye. Gisela Konopka, a major contributor to social group work and working with young people, encouraged workers to "listen to the cry of young people to be a person, not a thing to be treated." She also cautioned against behavior modification programs that deteriorate into mechanistic rituals failing to meet the needs of the young people.

Competence

The pioneers of group care saw their core responsibility to build competence and relationships by having positive expectations for young people. As early as 1833, M. Wicheren in Germany at the Rauhe Haus, wanted children "to feel at home in a well-developed family system of care and develop the faith that they could do something, be something, and own something" (Balbernie, 1972, p. 22). An article by John Watson (1896) describes the children and the first industrial school opened by Sheriff Watson in Scotland in 1841:

As individuals they had no love for school, for lessons, or control of any description… The new school, however, possessed very different features from those they had heard of or experienced; there were rumours of substantial breakfasts and dinners and suppers to be had after lessons; and there were also whispers of instruction in the arts of tailoring, shoemaking, and net making, and possibly even carpenter work, printing and book binding for the older boys—all trades which the youngest of them knew to be money making and therefore, desirable acquirements…

—Watson, 1896, pp. 257-258.

In 1913, Floyd Starr founded Starr Commonwealth in Michigan with the creed: "We believe there is no such thing as a bad boy, that badness is not a normal condition, that every boy will be good if given an opportunity in an environment of love and activity," emphasizing the need for relationships and opportunities to do something positive (Brendtro, 1990, p. 84). In Poland, Janusz Korczak set up an institute of youth government in his children's institution during the early 20th Century, empowering young people to gain competence and confidence. Father Flanagan instituted a student government at Boys Town, Nebraska, in 1926, allowing the boys to have a say and develop skills. Nicholas Hobbs, the father of the Re-ED movement in the 1970s, felt that competence and confidence in one's ability to be competent were essential to effective living.

Interaction with the Environment

Bruno Bettleheim (1950), at the University of Chicago Orthogenic School, stressed an environmental or ecological approach. He felt that it was just not enough to love children, but that one must also consider the impact of regular contact with the staff, the benefit of routines and transitions, as well as the activities and the educational advantages in the particular setting. Fritz Redl (1952), at the Pioneer House in Detroit, outlined a continuum of interventions beginning with the least intrusive, such as environmental control and structure, to ones that require a high degree of interaction and expectations. He also introduced the concept of the Life Space Interview, a process that he described as "the clinical exploitation of life's events" designed to use what happened in the immediate environment or "life space" to promote new coping strategies for the youth (Redl & Wineman, 1952).

Meeting Developmental Needs

Al Trieschman supported the use of a therapeutic milieu building on the work of Aichorn, Bettleheim, and Redl and "a general theory of how child growth and development can be supported and nourished by adults who care about and for children. Helping children in residential care does not need to be a special treatment for disturbed children to be phased into their lives by highly trained and dedicated adults" (Trieschman, Whittaker & Brendtro, 1969, p. vi).

Larry Brendtro at Starr Commonwealth wrote, "It has been our theses that the most effective programs for troubled youth entail a holistic synergy which results from skillfully harmonizing many important variables" (Brendtro & Ness, 1983, p. 178). He felt that the youth workers who could develop strong bonds with children ultimately were the most successful. Much like the early pioneers, Brendtro stressed relationship building, environmental support, and Life Space Interviews as some of the keys to successful work with emotionally and behaviorally troubled youth, helping them to grow and develop into healthy, competent adults.

Best Practice Guidelines Today

In 2001, the Child Welfare League of America (CWLA) convened a best practice task force of experts and professionals. The finished product, *CWLA Best Practice Guidelines: Behavior Management*, begins with an ethical and legal framework, followed by the critical role the administration and leadership play in the establishment of an organizational culture that promotes the growth and development of emotionally and behaviorally disturbed youth. Modeling appropriate ways for dealing with problems, developing a caring relationship with the youth, building relationships, listening and communicating, and developing and implementing activity programs were among the strategies listed.

In the United Kingdom, the 2003 Green Paper, *Every Child Matters*, written in consultation with children, families, and care workers, listed that what every child needs in residential care is an opportunity to:

- be healthy,
- stay safe,
- enjoy and achieve,
- make a positive contribution, and
- have economic well-being.

While residential care continues to evolve from warehousing children in some centers to meeting the special emotional, physical, and developmental needs of children in others, it is important to keep in the forefront what the pioneers have long known:

In all actions concerning children, whether undertaken by the public or private social welfare institutions, courts of law, administrative authorities or legislative bodies, the best interests of the child shall be a primary consideration.

—Article 3(1), United Nations Convention on the Rights of the Child (1989). ✿

CHAPTER 3
It Begins with What You Believe

Alice came to a fork in the road.
"Which road do I take?" she asked.
"Where do you want to go?" responded the Cheshire cat.
"I don't know," Alice answered.
"Then," said the cat, "it doesn't matter."

—Lewis Carroll, Alice in Wonderland

What do I do when…? This question comes up daily in residential care. How can knowledge be applied in day-to-day practice? A strong coherent approach to working with children and young people will guide decisions and interactions throughout the organization. Without a clear philosophical base from which to make a decision, it is hard to know which road to take. With a clear framework for care there is a foundation (or road map) on which to make a decision and choose an approach when deciding what to do in each situation. Beliefs about how children change and what they need are communicated through sets of principles that all staff members adhere to when interacting with young people. If the approach is not congruent throughout the agency, the impact of care will be diminished through inconsistencies and contradictions in actions taken by staff. This is not to say that everyone has to do exactly the same thing, at the same time, in the same way. A variety of techniques can be used by individual care workers, but all interventions and interactions need to adhere to the same set of principles.

Basic Principles of CARE

This program is founded on the following principles and beliefs about working with children in residential care:

Developmentally focused. The past two decades of resiliency research (focusing on the ability to succeed in spite of adversity or trauma) and long-term developmental studies of youth in high-risk environments have indicated that, "Resiliency is a capacity all youth have for healthy development and successful learning" (Benard, 2004, p. 4). All children have the same basic requirements for growth and development, but progress varies from child to child, in part, based on life experiences. Children in care need support and opportunities that engage their innate capacity to grow and develop. A main objective in residential care is to enhance the child's chances for normal development (Hawkins-Rodgers, 2007; Maier, 1987, 1991).

While all children need the same basic experiences and opportunities to develop into adulthood, children in care may need additional support and healing experiences in order to overcome life experiences that impeded their development. From this perspective, unusual behavior is viewed in terms of where it fits into the child's developmental progression instead of being viewed as "deviant or defiant behavior" (Bronfenbrenner, 1979). Development occurs by small steps and within the context of events (Elkind & Wiener, 1978). If a child does not have decisionmaking skills, it is critical to model decisionmaking skills, provide opportunities for the child to make decisions, and value those decisions once made.

Strategies for change are more effective when they match the child's present level of functioning. Children learn best when material and skills are presented that challenge the child to try new things, but do not overwhelm the child. This is referred to as the child's "zone of proximal development" (Vygotsky, 1978). This zone is defined in terms of the tasks that are difficult for the child to do alone, but can be accomplished with assistance. By (1) teaching new skills in deficit areas, (2) creating opportunities for the child to practice these new skills with adult assistance, and (3) adapting the environment so the child can succeed, care workers can orchestrate learning opportunities for children and adolescents to develop competencies in important areas. In the residential setting, a care worker can meet a child's developmental requirements within the context of daily events to help the child progress in managing life's challenges.

Family involved. The family of every child in care is an irremovable part of that child's life irrespective of circumstances. The child's ethnic, racial, and cultural identity is tied to the child's family. One of the goals of the residential experience is to strengthen family relationships. Children need permanent ties to caring and nurturing adults. Involving a parent or other concerned adult in the child's care and treatment, as well as planning adequate supports for the child's return to the community, are two of the few indicators of "successful treatment" with empirical validation (Curry, 1991; USGAO, 1994; Whittaker & Pfeiffer, 1994). These outcome studies underscore the need for contact and involvement with the family during and after placement. Family-focused residential care obtains the most positive child outcomes (Barth, 2005; Barth, Greeson, Guo, Green, Hurley, & Sisson, 2007). Helping children write letters home, arranging for contact with siblings, and planning for successful weekend stays at home are some examples of how care workers can support the child's relationship to the family.

Relationship based. The most significant task in residential care work is for staff to develop a trusting relationship with each child in their care. The relationships and attachments formed in the milieu are central to helping children develop competencies and form meaningful relationships throughout their lives (Fahlberg, 1990; Hawkins-Rodgers, 2007; Maier, 1991). Nurturing care experiences and basic attachments are necessary for children to grow into healthy adulthood. Through building alliances with adults, children can learn to trust, feel safe, develop relationships, and obtain the assistance they need in overcoming obstacles and solving problems. A person's ability to form relationships and positive attachments to others is an essential personal strength and manifestation of resiliency associated with healthy development and success in life (Benard, 2004; Goleman, 1998; Masten, 2004). Relationships also increase care staff's influence over and effectiveness in helping children learn interpersonal skills (Hubble, Duncan, & Miller, 1999; Trieschman et al., 1969). When faced with a difficult situation, such as children refusing to go to school, the children are more likely to respond and cooperate with an adult with whom they have a good relationship.

Competence centered. Competence is the combination of skills, knowledge, and attitude that each child needs to negotiate effectively with everyday life. In residential work, the care worker must help children become competent in managing their environment, as well as motivate them to cope with challenges and master new skills (Maluccio, 1991; Reiter & Bryen, 1991). If building social competence and other life skills is the goal, all interactions and activities become purposeful and process focused. Adults are concerned with helping the young people through the process so that they can develop new skills and insights into managing life's challenges and events—the means are as important as the end. For example, if two children are sharing a room and fighting over space, it is equally important to help the children resolve their interpersonal conflict and work out their differences, as it is to stop the fighting. Resolving conflicts is a critical life skill.

Learning to solve problems and developing flexibility, critical thinking skills, and insight are necessary for children if they are to overcome adversity and work things out (Benard, 2004). Helping children achieve personal goals and increasing their motivation to learn new skills are major tasks for care workers.

Trauma informed. A large percentage of children in residential care have a history of violence, abuse, and neglect resulting in debilitating effects on their growth and development (Abramovitz & Bloom, 2003; Bloom, 1997; Garbarino, 1999; Lieberman & Knorr, 2007; Perry & Pollard, 1998). Recent research on trauma has resulted in new understandings of children's challenging and difficult behaviors. All activities, routines, expectations, and interactions should be designed taking into account the impact of overwhelming stress and trauma on a child's development.

Maintaining an environment with a culture of nonviolence and safety is essential if children are to feel safe and are to learn new responses to stressful situations. Staff must shift their thinking about children from, "What is wrong with you?" to "What happened to you?" (Bloom, 1997, p. 191). If caregivers understand what has happened to children and comprehend the effects of violence, power, and control on their development, it helps keep the milieu focused on providing order and learning experiences versus demanding compliance and control.

This program is designed to help children who have experienced trauma develop into successful adults by fostering the child's innate capacity for healthy development. Resiliency is within the child and around the child. Children will learn what is around them through the adult models, the culture, and direct experience.

Ecologically oriented. Children and young people are continuously engaged in dynamic transactions with their environment in order to grow and develop (Bronfenbrenner, 1979; Maluccio, 1991). Various environmental opportunities are necessary to promote each child's effort to grow and develop. When children live in a community with caring adults who communicate their belief in the child's own strengths and abilities, children are motivated to learn, and their innate drive to grow and develop is fostered (Benard, 2004).

Caring and supportive environments provide children with a model of how to care for themselves and others (Swick, 2007). An underlying assumption in residential care is that environmental supports should be matched to the child's needs and changing qualities to maximize the child's growth and development. When the child is not progressing, it is as important to look at the child's environment as it is to look at the child for the solution. It is much easier and more reasonable to change the approach or manipulate the environment or activity, than to demand that the child make a change that may not be within his or her capacity to do so. For example, if a child is unable to get up and get ready for school in the 45 minutes allowed in the general schedule, wake the child up 15 minutes earlier.

The two most critical aspects of a group setting are the physical and social features that enable and encourage the child to participate in a variety of activities with children, adults, and alone. The more the environment can be enhanced to motivate the children to participate in more complex activities and relationships, the more opportunities for growth and development (Bronfenbrenner, 1979).

Summary

An organization with a clear philosophy of care lays the groundwork for all staff members to work cohesively in the best interests of the children in their care. This program is based on the principles of developmentally focused, ecologically oriented, competence centered, family involved, relationship based, and trauma informed. These principles cover not only the child's physical and emotional needs, but aim to teach children the most functional ways to interact with their environments. Though each child and each situation is different, an adherence to solid principles of care will guide an organization in making decisions that are in the best interest of every child. ✿

THE IMPORTANCE OF CARING

CHAPTER *4*

CHAPTER *4*

The Importance of Caring

Too often we underestimate the power of a touch, a smile, a kind word, a listening ear, an honest compliment, or the smallest act of caring, all of which have the potential to turn a life around.

—Leo Buscalgia

Care workers are the most important part of the young person's environment in residential care. The quality of relationships and interactions between the care workers and the young people determines whether the atmosphere is one of caring or one of stress.

One reason children and young people are often referred to residential care versus foster care is their inability to handle intense reciprocal relationships. That level of intimacy in a foster family setting is sometimes too much for the young people to manage with all of the other stressors in their lives. Children and young people who are scarred by a history of neglect, and/or emotional, physical, or sexual abuse often perceive adult-child relationships as adversarial and fraught with danger. Their ability to form attachments has been damaged along with their ability to trust adults because of these experiences (Fahlberg, 1990; Hawkins-Rodgers, 2007; Swick, 2007; Zegers, Schuengel, Van IJzendoorn, & Janssens, 2008). It may be almost too much to expect children and young people who have suffered so severely from broken and insecure attachments to ever trust fully in one person again. The most they may be able to manage is attaching to a place or a group (Ainsworth, 1999; Fahlberg, 1991; Lanyado, 2001; Schofield & Beek, 2005).

Residential care offers a variety of possible relationships and role models that can provide young people with opportunities to enhance their capacity and ability to form attachments and develop personal relationships. Young people have opportunities to choose attachment figures from numerous and diverse staff members.

Promoting Healthy Attachments

An attachment is a lasting connection between human beings that gives one the assurance of the other's continued presence and support even though the people involved might not be in direct contact with each other. "Attachment continues to persist over space, time, and other ongoing associations and foster independent autonomous existence, and the slow emergence of a sense of self" (Maier, 1994, p. 36). During placement, caregivers will need to attend to two critical tasks so that the children and young people can form important attachments: (1) supporting the child's enduring attachment to his or her family while (2) helping children cope with grief and loss after physically separating from their families or previous attachments.

The Importance of Family

Research on children and young people in placement shows the importance of parents, family, and the home environment (Curry, 1991; Fanshel & Shinn, 1978; Maluccio & Sinanoglu, 1981;

USGAO, 1994; Weiner & Weiner, 1990; Whittaker & Pfeiffer, 1994). The involvement of the family is important in predicting a successful discharge outcome. Therefore, efforts must be made to honor and strengthen that attachment. The family is a continuing reality for the child, regardless of the amount of contact, and must be taken into consideration throughout placement.

The Importance of Attachments

Attachment, separation, and loss are major themes for children in residential care. The experiences that children have in attaching to primary caregivers, separating from primary caregivers, and losing family, friends, school, home, pets, belongings, and so on, with each placement have a profound effect on their ability to trust and form relationships with adults. In order to learn to regulate effect, manage behavior, achieve autonomy and self-reliance, and develop a sense of self, a child must have confidence in and feel secure with an adult. Only with this security can the child feel free to explore, play, and learn. The adult provides a secure base when the child feels threatened, afraid, or stressed.

A child who is attached to one person can more easily become attached to others. In order to be autonomous while being dependent and trustful, one must have the ability to form healthy attachments to other human beings. In residential care, the young person will need to trust and rely on care workers to achieve developmental goals and build competencies. Through forming these alliances with care workers, children and young people learn to develop coping skills, social skills, and healthy relationships. They are then more able to form positive attachments to others in their next placement and throughout their adult lives.

Support the child's enduring attachment to his or her family. The family is the most important attachment in a child's life. Helping children feel secure in their attachment to their parents regardless of separation will help them manage other relationships. This attachment can be supported with opportunities for personal contact and/or information and knowledge about biological parents, siblings, and family. Regardless of the reasons for separation, children who possess adequate and favorable knowledge about absent parents and siblings are likely to have an enhanced sense of connectedness and well-being (Owusu-Bempah & Howitt, 1997).

Positive parental information is an important factor in children's overall adjustment, whereas devaluation of a parent diminishes a child's sense of trust in the world (Erikson, 1950; Owusu-Bempah & Howitt, 1997). It is important to speak respectfully of a child's family and to advance a feeling of connectedness to family and culture. Regardless of whether a child will ever return to his or her biological family to live, the family will always be an important influence in that child's life.

Helping children cope with their grief and loss after physically separating from their families or previous attachments is an importance care worker task. Children will have major difficulties progressing in care if they cannot form new attachments. By facilitating the grief process, the factors that work against forming new attachments are lessened. Encouraging and allowing children to express their strong emotions is key in developing attachments. Helping children deal with separation and loss and express these feelings is an attachment building opportunity.

How Attachments Are Formed

There are three primary ways that attachments are formed: (1) the arousal-relaxation cycle, (2) the positive interaction cycle, and (3) inclusion or claiming. All three methods have relevance for group care work. Group care must be structured so that the care workers' primary and central task is to provide for the immediate support, nurturance, and dependency of the children and young people in their care (Maier, 1982). To survive, all human beings must have air, water, food, and so on. These are basic physical needs. Children have these basic needs plus specific ones that must be met for healthy growth and development. Meeting a child's basic physical and safety needs is an important place to start.

The Arousal-Relaxation Cycle

Bowlby (1970) identified two characteristics of interactions between parents and children that affected the kind of attachment that developed. These characteristics are the speed and intensity of the parent's response to the child's discomfort. This attachment cycle begins when the child is an infant. Figure 1 depicts a successful interaction between the infant and caregiver. This interaction is initiated by the child. The child has a need, becomes stressed or

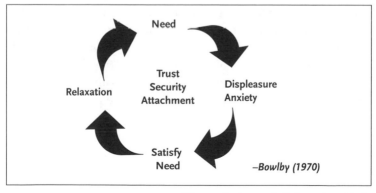

Figure 1. Arousal-Relaxation Cycle

tense, and lets the caregiver know by crying, squirming, moving about, turning red, and so on. It is crucial that the caregiver is sensitive to and responds quickly to meet the child's needs to alleviate the discomfort and to complete the cycle, thereby relaxing the child. If this cycle is completed repeatedly and consistently, the child learns to trust the caregiver and to feel secure. The world is a place that is safe and adults are people to trust.

When the child feels a need and the need is not met or is not met consistently, there is no release of tension. The child continues to feel anxious or even fearful and, eventually, the child becomes insecure, mistrustful, and unattached. There are many factors that can contribute to a broken cycle. The adult might be neglectful, abusive, or inconsistent; the child might be difficult to satisfy or be unable to express needs. It is important to remember the last step in the cycle—relaxation—that leads to attachment.

In residential care, older children can be helped in forming attachments to care workers by having the care workers provide support for physical and psychological or emotional needs. Cooking a special meal, supplying soft blankets, allowing for private space, and braiding or washing hair are just a few ways to provide physical comfort. Being supportive and empathic when a child is upset allows the child to express emotions and consequently relax. Accompanying an anxious child to a meeting or appointment or into an unknown situation gives comfort. The task of the caregiver is to experiment: to determine which interactions will soothe, comfort, and encourage the child to relate to others. The more difficult it is to relate to the child, the more the child needs to be encouraged to relate to others (Greenspan, 1999). This is the challenge for good childcare practice and is in the best interests of the child.

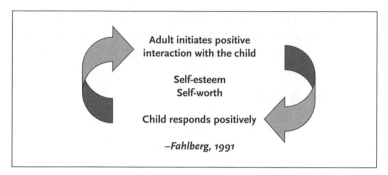

Figure 2. Positive Interaction Cycle

The Positive Interaction Cycle

Social interactions are as important as meeting basic needs as they stimulate growth and change (Ainsworth, 1967; Fahlberg, 1991; Howes, 1999). With the arousal-relaxation cycle, the child initiates the interaction by expressing a need and the caregiver feels competent in meeting the child's needs, thereby encouraging the building of an attachment (Fahlberg, 1991). In the positive interaction cycle, (Figure 2) the caregiver often initiates the interaction, a social interaction, by playing games, having a chat, or showing interest; the child feels lovable and worthwhile—two important components of building positive self-worth. In this interaction cycle, the child or the adult can start the interaction. Again, it is important that the cycle is completed.

The positive interactions can be as low key as "Good morning," or "How was your day at school?" Helping with homework or a chore, or playing a game are all ways to initiate a positive interaction. Children can also initiate these exchanges by asking for help or to spend some time with a care worker. These interactions are important ways to build trust and attachments and contribute to the child's feelings of self-worth. With a storehouse of these interactions, trust and the relationship are developed and can be drawn upon in times of crisis or upset.

Inclusion or Claiming

Including the child in the group, helping the child become part of "us" is a third way to form attachments (Fahlberg, 1990, 1991). This is an attachment to a family or group as demonstrated by the variety of groups to which people commonly feel a connection, such as their professional, political, or ethnic group. In the case of families, the parents start the claiming or inclusion process by finding similarities to them (such as, "he has my eyes, your nose"). With groups, inclusion entails meeting the criteria to *belong* to the group (such as, having the appropriate educational credentials, beliefs, or heritage). In group care, this claiming or inclusion into the group can be an important aspect of building attachments. Sharing experiences, rituals, and knowledge, as well as focusing on similarities rather than differences, helps facilitate this process. These are all ways of helping the child become part of *we* or *us*.

Building Attachments: Relationships with Caring Adults

Forming positive attachments with caring adults serves multiple purposes for children's development. Not only is the process of forming attachments necessary to meet basic needs for survival as an infant, this process is the basis for learning to regulate emotions. It provides a secure base for children to explore their environment and achieve developmental tasks. Being in the company of a competent caregiver reduces a child's fear in a new or challenging situation and allows the child to explore with confidence (providing a secure base) and manage stress. Disagreeing and having conflicts with competent caregivers helps children develop empathy and conflict resolution skills. These disagreements and discussions about values help the child develop a conscience. Relationships shape the development of self-awareness, social competence, conscience, emotional growth and regulation, and cognitive growth. Fostering strong, stable, and healthy relationships between children and their caregivers is a primary goal for care workers.

Co-Regulation and Self-Regulation Skills

Within the context of their relationships with adults, children learn to control their behavior, emotions, and attention—a skill set known as self-regulation (Cicchetti & Tucker, 1994; Gardner, Dishion, & Connell, 2008; Gestsdottir & Lerner, 2008). Ability to direct attention, shift the focus of attention, regulate emotions, and demonstrate socially acceptable behavior is fundamental to successful functioning in society. Children develop their abilities to regulate their emotions through interactions with adult caregivers who calm and soothe them. This process is called co-regulation (Bath, 2008; M. J. Holden et al., 2009). Infants need the presence of a caring adult to communicate soothing messages in order to learn to manage their own emotions. When a baby gets uncomfortable and stressed, the caregiver responds by holding or rocking the baby, cooing and smiling, helping the baby to relax and calm down. Adults manage babies' stress for them and through this co-regulation process children eventually learn to soothe themselves. As caregivers start identifying emotions for their children and helping them learn ways to manage those emotions, self-regulation skills are developed (Gerhardt, 2004; van der Kolk, 2005). Children who have not learned to manage their emotions will need adults to help them co-regulate (identify and manage) emotions throughout the day, as well as during times of stress and upset. ✿

CHAPTER 5
Providing a Secure Base

Every child needs at least one person who is really crazy about him (or her).

—*Urie Bronfenbrenner*

Instead of judging children's behavior as good or bad, inappropriate or appropriate, it is helpful to look at what is commonly referred to as *attention-seeking behavior* as *attachment-seeking behavior*. These behaviors are children's attempts to meet their needs for a secure and caring relationship with a nurturing adult.

Children with a history of insecure, anxiety-prone, or ambivalent attachments may express these needs in extreme ways by constantly hugging and touching care workers, ignoring a care worker completely, or even displaying violent behavior toward caregivers (Maier, 1994; Zegers et al., 2008). It is important to remember that these children have had neglectful and/or abusive experiences when attempting to attach to their caregivers. These children's failure to get their basic needs met has resulted in a negative view of the world and adults. They may need more attention and reassurance than most children, displaying attachment-seeking behaviors such as clinging to the adult, asking silly questions, interrupting conversations, and so on.

When these children are not reassured they may respond aggressively. They may distance themselves or may even appear to be indifferent to the care worker. All of these responses, although frustrating and irritating to care workers, are protective mechanisms children have developed based on their previous experiences. If these behaviors are viewed as cries to form attachments, there are countless opportunities throughout the day to give children a second chance to experience a nurturing, reciprocal relationship. Forming trusting relationships and positive attachments to others are necessary skills for social competence (Benard, 2004; Goleman, 1995).

Meeting Basic Needs

Children and young people, regardless of where they live and whom they live with, all have the same basic requirements for personal care, social interaction, intellectual stimulation, hope, creativity, and a sense of belonging. Nurturing care experiences are necessary for all children and young people, but are critical for children and young people who lack secure roots and have suffered traumatic experiences (Bronfenbrenner, 1979; Maier, 1991; Swick, 2007). It is in the milieu that their basic needs are met, trust is developed, and attachments are formed.

Care workers are the crucial link between children in care and their ability to benefit from the care experience (Moses, 2000; Rosen, 1999). Children need to be able to rely upon and attach to an adult in order to feel confident enough to take risks and venture out on their own. A good example of this behavior is a toddler who will explore new playground equipment or enter a sandbox with other children as long as *mommy* is in sight. Having the *secure base* in view gives the toddler the courage and security to risk new experiences.

Children have positive attachments to adults who are highly responsive in meeting their basic needs and providing nurturance. A good place to start is meeting basic dependency needs, such as food, shelter, and clothing, and meeting them in a way that feels good. When looking at basic needs, care workers can use Maslow's (1969) hierarchy of needs to help assess children's needs and behaviors and structure their time and efforts to provide dependency support and nurturance (Figure 3).

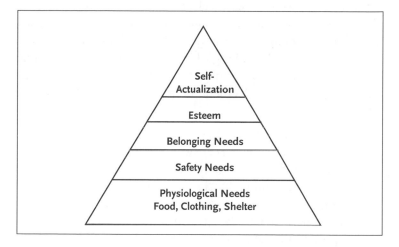

Figure 3. Maslow's Heirarchy of Needs

Since this is a hierarchy, it is important to make sure the lowest level needs are met first and continually, so that the individual can move on to higher level needs. Maslow saw all of these needs as survival needs if an individual is to have a healthy, meaningful life. If someone has had problems with one level, such as not having enough food to eat or experiences of being physically abused, that person may fixate on that need and worry about having enough to eat or being safe even when there is plenty of food in the house or when they are in a safe relationship. In addition, everyone tends to regress to a lower level when under stress or in a threatening situation. Meeting children's needs in caring and nurturing ways is a perfect opportunity to build healthy attachments and provide reparative attachment experiences for children in care.

Doing With, Not To

Daily care events such as mealtimes, bed and wake-up times, chores, leisure activities, personal care, and snack times are attachment-building opportunities. Sitting side-by-side during a movie, spontaneously making a bowl of popcorn, helping a child make the bed, braiding a child's hair: all are examples of a care worker's personal involvement in meeting children's physical needs.

Personal involvement in children's physical care is the base for building attachments. As care workers do things *with* the children, instead of doing things *to* the children, ordinary interactions become the building blocks of positive attachments. Instead of standing back and supervising, care workers are engaged with the children in their activities. During these activities, care workers can provide the support necessary for children to be successful, lowering hurdles and allowing children to achieve mastery instead of simply supervising and doling out consequences when children fail to achieve. Care workers can structure activities within the child's zone of proximal development more successfully if they are doing the activity with the child.

Responding, Not Reacting

Attachment behaviors, often referred to as attention-seeking behaviors, represent a child's efforts to attach to caregivers and build relationships. When questions such as, "When do we eat?", "What are we doing this afternoon?", and actions such as demanding to go outside, get a snack, or buy a CD, are viewed as attempts to attach instead of behaviors to be dealt with, the care worker will respond to meet the need versus react to discourage the expression of the need. This approach is relationship based and developmentally focused, but is not easily achieved. It requires skill and a great deal of sensitivity and patience.

Attachment Building Responses

How care workers think about and behave toward children are fundamental factors in the likelihood of children becoming positively attached to them. Care worker behaviors and characteristics that promote the forming of attachments include availability, sensitivity, acceptance, and investment (Howes, 1999; Howe, Brandon, Hinings, & Schofield, 1999; Maier, 1994; Schofield & Beek, 2005). These are the qualities that help children learn to trust adults.

Availability. Children need to trust that the care worker is available and ready to assist them. This is more than merely being present; it is being actively involved in helping children manage their daily lives. Being available and involved in the child's life must be a positive experience for both the child and the adult. Meeting children's needs when they express the need instead of when it seems *appropriate* or convenient for the staff or the program is often difficult to manage. Support from the organization is essential in making *availability* a primary task for care workers. Even when not present, care workers can communicate their availability by letting the child know that *he was on their mind*. Bringing in a magazine or picture that reminded the care worker of the child promotes trust in the availability of the care worker.

Sensitivity. Care workers need to respond sensitively to the children's urgent cries for satisfaction, acknowledge the stress the child is experiencing, and try to meet the need, thus completing the arousal-relaxation cycle. It also requires that the care worker is sensitive to the child and the child's way of communicating needs. Knowing when a child needs a snack, a hug, or a safe activity by being sensitive to and knowledgeable of a child's behavior helps strengthen a child's attachment to adults.

Acceptance. It is important for care workers to recognize children's attachment behavior as attempts to belong and to be included. Maintaining an open attitude and accepting children for who they are and as partners in their care and treatment, facilitates the child's ability to build a sense of self and competence. Care workers must be prepared to overlook inappropriate behavior at times, communicate unconditional acceptance, and encourage the child to try again in the name of promoting positive attachments. Having fun during menial tasks communicates to the child that they are a pleasure to be around.

Investment. The thoughts and feelings that care workers have about the children influence how they behave with the children. Care workers must take pride in the children and believe in their future possibilities. When care workers have confidence in the children's abilities and what they can be, children have greater confidence in themselves. Children learn to forgive themselves and try again when adults model acceptance and personal investment for the children in their care. Having high expectations for children helps children believe in themselves and have hope for the future.

Daily care routines and events are fertile grounds for building attachments. Helping meet children's basic needs in a caring and nurturing way helps establish trusting relationships and provides the groundwork for solving difficult problems and over-coming obstacles in the future. This is where care begins.

Summary

The relationships between workers and children in care are key to the success of the residential placement. An advantage of residential care for children who have had trouble with relationships in the past is the variety of relationships offered within the setting. Attachments to workers, other children, and to place are essential if children are to learn emotional and physical self-regulation. Care workers must also strive to maintain a child's attachments to his or her family and community in order for the child to develop a secure sense of self. Attachments may be gained through several avenues: the arousal-relaxation cycle, in which a child's need is satisfied by a caregiver, leading to relaxation; the positive interaction cycle, in which positive social interaction between a child and adult leads to positive feelings on both ends; and inclusion or claiming, in which a child is included in and feels part of a group. Attachment is one of the most basic and vital developmental goals of a child. Care workers should strive to provide opportunities for all children to become involved in positive individual and group relationships. A care worker can best serve a child's needs by determining what each child's particular behaviors mean in terms of their needs, and then responding with availability, sensitivity, acceptance, and investment. The more consistently a worker can meet the needs of the children in their care, the more likely the children are to feel a sense of attachment to the worker and begin to trust in the worker and in themselves. ✿

CREATING AN ENVIRONMENT WHERE CHILDREN CAN THRIVE

CHAPTER 6

Creating a Therapeutic Milieu

When you plant lettuce and it doesn't grow well, you don't blame the lettuce.

—*Thich Nhat Hahn, Vietnamese Buddhist monk*

Children do well if they can, (Greene & Ablon, 2006, p. 186) and if they cannot, the job of the organization and every residential care worker is to provide an environment where children can succeed. The factors in the environment to consider include the physical environment, routines, activities, instruction, opportunities to participate and contribute, and the quality of relationships with adults and children.

Therapeutic Milieu

The heart of residential care is the milieu. The milieu is the environment where structure, activities, and interactions take place. "The milieu is the surrounding or environment that someone lives in and is influenced by" (*The Encarta World English Dictionary*, 2006). In residential settings, the milieu is the place where attachments form, trust grows, relationships develop, and the foundation for growth and change is laid. It is essential that the organization's program philosophy be evident in daily activities, routines, and interactions throughout the milieu. The therapeutic milieu is only effective when all elements of the environment work together consistently to influence a child's growth and development (Fahlberg, 1990). Positive child and youth development depends on the quality of the milieu.

The Ecology of a Caring Environment

Ecological *thinking* focuses on the give and take or reciprocity between people and their environment—how they interact within their environment. People change their physical and social environments and are changed by them though a process of continuous reciprocal adaptations. When everything goes well, these adaptations support the growth and development of the person and enrich the environment (Germain & Gitterman, 1996).

It is generally within the milieu that children face their greatest frustrations and fears. Children placed in residential care usually have a history of low achievement and failing to meet demands in other settings. Within the residential setting, the milieu can be structured so that young people can succeed within their abilities. Additionally, the youth have the opportunity to experience positive solutions to conflicts and problems rather than repeat the predominantly negative experiences from the past. Residential care agencies must establish a balance between what the environment demands and the child's ability to respond to those demands. The environment should be structured in a way that meets each child's needs and maintains a sense of order. Developmentally appropriate practice is based on the use of a variety of individual strategies to meet the specific needs of each child. This takes flexibility and teamwork. Inflexible point and level systems that focus on earning or losing activities and do not allow for individual adaptation are often counterproductive to a therapeutic milieu (Mohr, Martin, Olson, Pumariega, & Branca, 2009; VanderVen, 2000). For the milieu to be an effective therapeutic tool, children and young people must have the opportunity to build relationships with adults and peers, and the environment must be carefully planned to provide realistic positive learning opportunities within the child's zone of proximal development.

Resiliency

How do so many children and young people overcome adversity and trauma in order to change their lives? Research on resiliency (the ability to succeed in spite of adversity or trauma) and child maltreatment has resulted in some significant findings for those who care for children who have experienced traumatic events (Benard, 2004; Masten, 2001; Zielinski & Bradshaw, 2006). Some children are able to develop into healthy functioning adults even though they have suffered traumatic experiences. The research has uncovered certain attributes or conditions and protective factors that exist for these children that have assisted them in overcoming the obstacles thrown in their path. Positive emotional relationships with competent and caring adults has been identified as one of the most important external or environmental protective factors (Siegel, 1999; Werner, 1990). If children have a stable, caring, supportive, and positive relationship with a primary adult caregiver, they are more able to withstand the damaging effects of traumatic events. Other attributes that contribute to children's resiliency include internal or personal strengths such as personal cognitive and self-regulation skills, self-confidence, social competence, autonomy, sense of purpose, problem-solving skills, and motivation to succeed (Benard, 2004; Gardner et al., 2008; Gestsdottir & Lerner, 2008; Masten, 2001). It is important to remember that resiliency is not absolute; everyone has a breaking point. Given enough trauma and risk factors such as poverty, punitive or emotionally unavailable parents/caregivers, and abusive treatment, even the most resilient children will succumb to emotional and behavioral problems.

Resiliency and Environmental Protective Factors

There are specific external factors in the environment that help protect children and young people from risk and tap into their innate potential for healthy growth and development. These environmental factors are caring relationships, high expectation messages, and opportunities for participation and contribution (Benard, 1991, 2004; Masten & Reed, 2002; Swick, 2007).

Caring relationships. Caring environments are created by the presence of caring adults. Caring relationships are characterized by trust, availability, acceptance, positive regard, and respect (Benard, 2004; Howe et al., 1999; Maier, 1994; Schofield & Beek, 2005). Being there for children is an important part of being a compassionate caregiver. Compassionate care workers do not take children's negative behavior personally, but look beneath the behavior and understand the needs. Forming attachments and developing caring relationships help meet children's needs and teach children how to meet other people's needs.

High expectation messages. Believing in children and young people, even when they do not believe in themselves, sends a message to them that they can achieve and be successful. Care workers who believe in children's abilities to succeed and are able to communicate this belief to children challenge them to reach their goals and realize their dreams. Building on a child's strengths, interests, and hopes motivates children to try and engages their innate capacities to learn and develop (Benard, 2004; Maier, 1994).

Opportunities for participation and contribution. When children are engaged in interesting and challenging activities, they have opportunities to learn, develop relationships, enjoy the sense of belonging to a group, be creative, and problem-solve. When they are participating, they are also contributing and giving something of themselves to others. By giving something to others, their sense of self-worth and self-efficacy is enhanced (Benard, 2004; Brendtro et al., 1998). Children and young people develop a sense of power, respect and meaning through participating in activities and contributing to others and the community.

When working from an ecological perspective, all parts of the environmental system strive to maximize the child's ability to gain competence and develop new skills and abilities. The milieu provides the opportunities and conditions that enable growth and development in children. It is a nurturing place that offers children comfort and security and enhances the care worker's capacity to nurture (Ainsworth, 1999). Secure attachments ultimately lead to a child's ability to be independent. A child who can choose whom to depend on, is a child who is both attached and free (Maier, 1982). ✿

CHAPTER 7

The Milieu Experience

We do not remember days, we remember moments.

—Cesare Pavese

The group living experience should be filled with opportunities for forming attachments, building relationships, and learning life skills. Children and adolescents progress developmentally when they can rehearse new and different ways of managing daily events, problem-solve when obstacles appear, and turn to supportive care workers for guidance and assistance.

One way to help children develop new life skills is to set expectations based on the needs of individual children at any given point in their placement. As previously discussed, high expectation messages foster children's development and help them overcome adverse circumstances (Benard, 2004). Expectations are developed based on the abilities of the child and the norms that are important to maintain for the entire group. Expectations are not rules. Rules are focused on keeping everyone safe.

Helping Children Meet Expectations

Setting and maintaining realistic expectations for children and young people is an important part of the developmental process. Sending high expectations messages, feeling positive and optimistic about the child's abilities, and communicating hope for the future are important ingredients in providing quality care (Benard, 2004; de Schipper, Riksen-Walraven, Geurts, & Derksen, 2007). At the center of caring relationships are clear and positive expectations. Creating an environment in which children can thrive entails setting up a structure and sending positive messages (such as, "You are a capable human being."). The focus is on the expectation and not the violation of the expectation. Expectations stand regardless of whether the child has met the expectation or not. When the expectation is not met, it does not become an issue of noncompliance, but a challenge for the care worker to help the child meet the expectation in the future. If the care worker's response is to deduct points, drop levels, or assign consequences when an expectation is not met, the focus becomes, "How to get the child to comply with the consequence instead of how to meet the expectation." The care worker's role is to help the child learn ways to meet expectations since they are important life skills. This helps avoid power struggles and shifts the concerns from who is in charge to how to help the child learn new competencies and be successful every day (Mohr et al., 2009; VanderVen, 2000).

A Rule About Rules

Rules, like routines, provide a predictable structure that establishes boundaries and minimal expectations for behavior. Unlike expectations, rules focus on providing safety and security for the children and staff. Rules are generally positive actions for people to take and when stated in the positive—what behavior is wanted; not what is not wanted—are clearer and easier to follow. For example, "Wear a seat belt when in the car." The fewer rules, the more flexibility the staff and team have to implement the responses and program services that are best for each individual child at any given time in placement. The more rules a program has, the more the care worker becomes an enforcer of rules rather than a caring professional trained to support, encourage, and teach the young people. Rules are an authoritarian approach to guide or control behaviors and work best when limited to safety and security concerns.

Order Versus Control

There is a difference between maintaining a sense of order and maintaining control. No one likes to be controlled, especially children in care who have very little control over the essential elements of their lives. It is important to maintain order and structure so that children and young people can function, build competencies, and develop more autonomy and independence. This can be accomplished without resorting to control tactics that often lead to power struggles and explosive behaviors. The following are strategies to assist the care worker in establishing and maintaining structure, routines, and expectations.

Communicating a Framework for Understanding

Early in a child's life, caregivers begin to communicate expectations and request compliance with safety rules. As infants and toddlers enter early childhood, adults ask that children adhere to family standards of behavior and cultural or social norms. As children learn these expectations through routines of daily life, they internalize these behaviors and conform to standards of behavior. This is the early development of self-control. Sensitive and sympathetic care giving, combined with firm and warm parenting styles, are associated with the development of self-control. Unfortunately, many children in care have had inconsistent care giving and contradictory messages and expectations.

"Communicating a framework for understanding with youth helps them to develop a sense of meaning and a sense of rationality within daily life" (Anglin, 2002, p. 127). Rules, routines, and expectations should be discussed, understood, and agreed upon by all who are affected. Asking children to follow instructions without question or reason is not only an abuse of power on the adult's part, but a lost opportunity to help the child build competencies in life skills. It is important to remember that trust is the foundation for everything. It begins by being clear about what the expectations are, why they are important, and making sure the child has the skills and support needed to be successful. Providing the support the child needs in order to guarantee success builds trust and self-efficacy. Trusting that the child will meet realistic expectations will help the child make positive choices.

Setting Expectations

Insuring success in meeting expectations begins by being clear about what the expectations are, why they are important, and making sure the child has the skills and support needed to be successful. When setting expectations, it is important to make sure they are reasonable and necessary for the child's healthy growth and development. There are several guidelines that can help set realistic expectations.

Reasonable and fair. Each child has individual needs and abilities. Being fair to a child does not mean treating everyone the same. Some children wake up easily ready to face the day, others drag themselves out of bed after several prompts. Some children eagerly approach new activities and are easily bored and ready to take on a new challenge. Other children resist transitions and need many reminders and time to prepare. Bedtime can be extra challenging since many children do not like quiet time alone with only their thoughts and memories. Setting expectations that meet the needs of individual children, are trauma-sensitive, and are within their zone of proximal development help create a therapeutic milieu.

Developmentally appropriate and competence centered. Children have different levels of ability based on where they are developmentally. If children are to learn, grow, and develop, expectations need to change as the child does. A care worker needs to be able to read each child's rhythm through body language, and verbal and nonverbal behaviors in order to provide the support and encouragement that the individual child needs to manage daily activities. Expectations should help children learn life skills and routines that will serve them well in adulthood. All expectations should have goals and a purpose that is in the best interest of the child.

Mutually agreed. Children are more motivated to meet expectations that they have personally helped to develop. Letting young people participate in setting their own expectations, helping them to learn to make good choices, and supporting their efforts at making better choices is a characteristic of a well-functioning residential care unit (Anglin, 2002). This is where flexibility and teaching come into the mix. If the goal of residential care is to *raise* competent, responsible young people, there must be opportunities for young people to learn how to be responsible and competent. This entails much more than quietly following orders or being punished for not following orders. Learning how to be responsible includes understanding the expectation, looking at options in meeting expectations, making decisions, taking action, and getting feedback.

Summary

Good residential care begins with a good foundation. The environment in which care is given can have major impacts on the children and caregivers who live, work and play there. Specific environmental factors that protect children from risk and foster healthy development are caring relationships, high expectation messages, and opportunities for participation and contribution.

Expectations and rules are not the same. Rules are for making sure the environment is safe, whereas having realistic expectations for children will guide them towards behaviors that are good for both the child and the residential environment. Care workers should strive to create order in the residential environment without exerting control tactics over the residents. Order can be maintained by communication with children about expectations, involving the children in setting their own expectations, making sure they are realistic, fair, and developmentally appropriate. When the children know that workers believe in them and are willing to assist them in making good choices, they have the tools they need to reach their potential. ✿

Responding To Trauma and Pain-Based Behavior

CHAPTER 8
Trauma and Pain-Based Behavior

It is easier to blame the victim than to deal with the cause.

—Anonymous

Imagine punishing a child for crying, screaming, and demanding attention after receiving a cut on the leg in a fall from a bicycle. No reasonable adult would do this. But many children are punished in schools, homes, and residential care when they express their emotional pain. No child should be punished for behavior that is a result of pain—either physical or emotional. That would be inflicting pain on top of the pain they already feel, which would only increase the damage.

Recent research on trauma, brain development, and cognitive, social, emotional, and behavioral functioning, has resulted in new understandings of children's challenging and difficult behaviors (Ledoux, 2002; Lieberman & Knorr, 2007; Perry, 2002b; van der Kolk, 1994). After intensely studying 10 group care facilities, Anglin identified many of the emotional and behavioral problems of youth in care as "pain-based behavior" (Anglin, 2002; Brendtro, 2004). The ability to deal with children and youth's psychological and emotional pain without inflicting additional painful experiences on them is one of the biggest challenges for care workers and those who work in residential care facilities.

What Is Trauma?

"Traumatization occurs when both internal and external resources are inadequate to cope with external threat" (van der Kolk & Ducey, 1989). Many people experience traumatic events, such as a car accident, a flood, the death of a loved one. Although most of these people experience great emotional pain and a period of disorganization or dysfunction, eventually they are able to return to normal functioning with or without some professional assistance.

Children with a history of abuse, neglect, abandonment, devaluation, and exposure to chronic family and/or neighborhood violence face a more complicated and debilitating situation. Depending on their age and the extent and duration of the threat, their brain development may be affected (Lieberman & Knorr, 2007; Perry, 1997; Schore, 2001). Trauma in childhood can permanently alter the way the brain functions. For example, when someone is under threat, the mind and body respond to the threat by either preparing to fight or flee. The brain is designed to sense, process, perceive, act upon, and store information from the internal and external world. When an internal condition such as thirst or dehydration or an external threat such as a stranger approaching quickly persists, this places stress on the system. The brain then adjusts the body's emotional (level of arousal), cognitive (style of thinking), and physiological states (heart rate, muscle tone, rate of respiration), in order to respond to the stress/threat. Once a person has quenched the thirst or the stranger has walked by, the stress is reduced, the body relaxes and returns to baseline. The more stressful or threatening the situation, the more regressed or primitive the thinking and behavior becomes as different parts of the brain control and organize the response. This is all part of the brain's stress response system designed to help people survive in hostile and threatening situations. It is a human's fight or flight mechanism.

As discussed earlier, low-level stress during a child's early years is necessary for healthy development. In the arousal-relaxation cycle, the child feels discomfort, cries, is comforted, and the child's stress is relieved through the co-regulation process. The child develops an attachment, a sense of security, and learns to trust. This enables the child to take risks and explore the world as he or she grows up. With a consistent, available, and safe caregiver as a base, the child learns how to cope with and regulate stress and emotions.

Dramatic, rapid, unpredictable, or threatening changes in the environment activate the stress response system. If these events are prolonged, chronic, or severe, the child's brain and body stay in this survival mode. During childhood when the brain is still developing, traumatic events such as exposure to violence or chronic abuse or neglect can result in changes to the brain so that the child is in a permanent state of arousal even when there is no threat.

Children who are exposed to violence often develop emotional, behavioral, thinking, psychosomatic, and sleeping disorders (Garbarino, 1999). These children may be impulsive, easily distracted with attention problems, or addicted to danger. They may perceive events that seem harmless to most people as if they presented a high level of danger. For example, a child walking past a table in the cafeteria bumps the table. Bobby's milk is spilt when the table is bumped. Bobby jumps up and hits the child who walked past. The other children thought it was an accident, Bobby perceived it as a hostile act. Eventually this condition can lead to many emotional and behavioral problems such as aggression, violence, self-injury, and/or substance abuse.

Living in a World with Violence

Even children in care who have not been abused and neglected have often been exposed to violence in the home, in the neighborhood, at school, or in the media. In many ways, violence is accepted as a legitimate way to resolve conflict in our society. It is prevalent in movies, on television, and in music. Although all children are susceptible to the harmful effects of violence, some are more vulnerable than others.

Children are more at risk if they experience multiple traumas, such as violence at home and on the streets. Some emotionally disabled children are also more vulnerable to soaking up the violence they see (Garbarino, 1995). Many of the children most exposed to violence and violent imagery already face serious developmental risks due to poverty, racism, neglect, devaluation, family instability, and drugs.

The effects of exposure to violence can emerge quickly or appear slowly over time. Children respond to violence in many different ways. Many young children are left feeling scared, hopeless, and unsafe—even in their own homes. Others may experience sleep disturbances, intrusive thoughts, emotional numbing, and diminished expectations for the future.

The trauma of violence can produce significant psychological problems that interfere with learning and appropriate social behavior in school. Children have difficulty learning when they are feeling afraid. Many children develop a pattern of aggressive behavior, which, if left unchecked, can lead to serious acts of violence. The experience of violence creates enormous challenges for children and the people who care for them (Garbarino & Holden, 1997).

Separation and Loss and Trauma

Separation and loss is a part of life. In fact, it is a necessary part of a child's development. With each stage of development, there is a gain and a loss. When children learn to walk, they gain mobility but lose the security of being held and carried by a parent. When children enter school they gain friends but lose the constant attention of an adult caregiver. At each step, the child experiences anxiety but with a consistent, caring, competent, and supportive caregiver, the child works through the feelings of loss and separation and adjusts to the new freedoms and opportunities. This is a normal, necessary part of life. Children's ability to separate and manage on their own is based on the security of their attachments combined with their skills to attach and interact with others and their environment.

When separations and losses are sudden, unexpected, dramatic, extreme, and/or repeated, they are essentially traumatic events. Children become overwhelmed with anxiety and may develop feelings of guilt, anger, shame, and helplessness. The ability of children to move through the grieving process depends on their age, the circumstance of the loss, their overall emotional level of functioning, and the support they receive. All children in residential care have experienced at least one loss by coming into residential care. Being able to understand and respond to children's expression of loss, as part of the grieving process, is a critical skill for care workers.

Tangible and Intangible Loss

Children and adolescents experience two types of losses. Tangible loss involves something physical (such as a loss of a pet, a home, a favorite toy). Intangible losses are mostly emotional or psychological and are more difficult to manage (such as a sense of safety, future, self-esteem, joy). Children in residential care are usually children who have suffered multiple and repeated losses, most of which have never been grieved or healed. When a loss remains unacknowledged and unmourned, it becomes devalued and dehumanized (Hardy & Laszloffy, 2005). As a result, the child feels devalued and unworthy. Children in out-of-home care live lives that are saturated with losses that go unacknowledged. Their loss and pain are often ignored and when they act out their pain, they may be punished. Sensitive care workers make themselves available to children to help them grieve their losses and move forward. ✿

CHAPTER 9

Identifying and Responding To Pain-Based Behavior

We need to shift our thinking from "What is wrong with you?" to "What happened to you?"

—Sandra Bloom

With the level of trauma children in residential care today have experienced, a *trauma informed approach* to care and treatment serves the best interests of the child. With this approach all programs, activities, services, and relationships take into account the overwhelming impact of stress, loss, and trauma on children's development. The organization creates a culture for healing which promotes positive change, maximizes strengths and minimizes weaknesses, and buffers children and adults from repetitive stress (Abramovits & Bloom, 2003). Environments, programs, and interactions are designed to mediate the effect that trauma has had on the children's lives.

Children Handle Trauma As Best They Can

In a threatening situation, the normal response is for the child to go to the adult caregiver for help. If no response is received (for example, the caregiver is absent, unresponsive, incapacitated by the threat, or the caregiver is the threat) the child soon abandons this strategy and generally responds in three ways: re-experiencing the trauma, hyperarousal, and dissociation or avoidance (Lieberman & Knorr, 2007; Perry & Pollard, 1998). These responses have profound effects on the child's future physical, emotional, and behavioral responses to perceived stressful situations.

Sometimes the child may re-enact the traumatic event. This may appear during play, in drawings, or behaviors. Some children, especially young children, engage in play that has a repetitive quality, repeating the trauma he or she experienced. For example, a child may play house and repeatedly punish the children or may tell a story about an *event* over and over. This re-enactment may be an attempt to gain control over the situation. Under stressful situations, the child may experience a flashback, a recurring memory, or a feeling or perceptual experience of a past event. The child feels as though he or she is re-experiencing the event as if it were happening right now. These types of responses can be triggered when the child feels a loss of control, is being restrained, is reminded of a traumatic event (consciously or unconsciously), or when a child feels threatened or vulnerable. Sometimes children may react with extreme distress to smells, sounds, or touches that they associate with a traumatic event. They may have nightmares and have trouble sleeping.

Children who dissociate may become detached, emotionally numb, and compliant, often with a decreased heart rate. They usually disengage from the circumstance and focus on internal stimuli. Essentially, they freeze as a rabbit does when it senses danger. When observing these children, they may look defeated or in a day dreaming state. They exhibit avoidant behaviors and may actually be immobilized in a threatening situation and experience short-term memory loss.

If hyperarousal is the response to threatening situations, the child initially experiences an alarm response that starts with anxiety, builds to fear, and then culminates in terror. If this response is triggered repeatedly, the child will eventually be fearful most of the time even when there is no threat—when the child is at baseline. These children are easily traumatized and may perceive threat in almost any circumstance. They often become aggressive, manipulative, defiant, oppositional, and inflexible. The result for all these children is that they have difficulties in forming relationships and they have problems calming themselves (self-soothing). They may also have additional behavioral and emotional problems.

Recognizing Pain-Based Behavior

Being able to read a child's behavior, seeing what is behind the behavior in terms of motive, intent, and feelings, is a skill that care workers can develop through reflective practice (Anglin, 2002). It is essential that care workers understand the meaning behind the children's troubling behaviors in order to respond effectively. Pain-based behavior takes many forms. Most commonly it appears as impulsive outbursts, aggressive acts, inability to tolerate uncertainty or ambiguity, withdrawing or running away, clinginess, and self-injury.

Each child will have triggers; some they are aware of and some they are not. Assisting children to identify their triggers will help them prepare for and avoid stressful situations. Care workers must look at the feelings behind the behavior. What is the child doing? How does the child look/feel? Answering these questions will assist the care worker in recognizing pain-based behavior. Once identified, care workers have many opportunities to assist children in managing these feeling and behaviors and promoting positive change.

Listen to the children talk about their feelings. Children need to talk about what is upsetting them. They need to talk and process the very same feelings and events many times. Even years after the trauma, they may still be struggling to understand why they cannot live at home, why their parents do not visit, why they were rejected, abandoned, abused. Listen respectfully and empathically to what the child is expressing. Encourage the expression of feelings and acknowledge the loss. Help the child understand the event as best they can. This is not therapy—this is listening to understand.

Watch for triggers or signs of *re-enactments* or flashbacks. Be supportive and try to identify patterns of behaviors and triggers to the behaviors. Re-enactments may appear as power struggles or unexplained crying or aggression. Comfort the child and help the child avoid these triggers in the future. During team meetings, staff can work to identify patterns of behaviors and triggers to these behaviors.

Give the child choices and a sense of control. When children feel they do not have control, they will likely have a stress reaction. When children are given control or choices, they will feel safer and more comfortable. They will be able to think more clearly and react in a more adaptive manner.

Teach children to express their emotions and resolve conflicts through discussion and negotiation. Learning to regulate emotions and solve problems are critical skills required to promote healthy development and to feel in control. They also will help the children have sense of a better future motivating them to move forward.

Helping children understand the past, develop self-regulation skills, and have a positive sense of the future, will assist them in overcoming past traumatic events. Although the pain from the past may never disappear, the more skills and abilities the child has to cope with the pain, the more optimistic the child is about the future. Future orientation and hope are necessary if children are going to invest in making positive changes.

Creating a Culture of Nonviolence

A culture of nonviolence is essential and is the responsibility of everyone in the residential organization, including adults and children. Safety is the essence of childhood and includes physical and emotional safety. As discussed previously, basic needs must be met so that children do not need to worry about food, shelter, clothing, or physical safety. Respectful communication and acknowledgement of each other's feelings helps build emotional and psychological security. Building trusting relationships and managing conflict and frightening situations by talking rather than fighting promotes a feeling of social safety. Everyone should feel safe enough to do the right thing and make good choices. Decisions should be value-based and respectful of each other and the community. Providing a safe and calm environment is integral to meeting the needs of traumatized children and youth. Some ways to accomplish this are:

(1)   Establish a consistent, predictable structure to the day. Meals, bedtimes, homework times, activity times, and chores should be at consistent times. When there are new or different activities, inform children in advance and explain the reasons for the variation. Care workers should avoid looking disorganized, confused, or anxious since children need to feel that adults are *in control*. Avoid the, *No one told me there was a change, I just work here*, attitude. Always communicate a sense of order and safety.

(2) **Provide a secure base.** When children feel threatened or afraid, they need an adult to whom they are attached to provide the secure base where they can return and get comfort and assurances (Lieberman & Knorr, 2007; Maier, 1982, 1987). In residential care, the young person will need to trust and rely on care workers to provide this secure base. Care workers need to develop positive attachments and caring relationships that model respect and compassion.

(3) **Discuss expectations, rules, and limits in advance so that children understand what is expected.** Use flexibility so that expectations are within the child's *zone of proximal development* in which learning and change is possible. Avoid power assertion whenever possible to reduce the appearance of a threat and to avoid triggering a stress response.

(4) **Avoid activities or events that may trigger the child's stress response.** Carefully choose movies, books, music, and activities that are calming. Avoid violent images. If an activity is upsetting or re-traumatizing for a child, stop the activity or adjust it to avoid escalating the situation. Protect the children.

(5) **Provide activities that promote future orientation such as caring for animals, plants, and people.** Allow children to make choices and imagine a different life. Create opportunities to make positive changes and envision a better future. Traumatized youth are likely to exhibit terminal thinking and have a sense of hopelessness.

Summary

No one should be exposed to events so overwhelmingly terrible that they cause trauma, yet many children in care have been affected by just such experiences. Not only have some children experienced abuse and neglect in their home, children also encounter violence in their neighborhoods, schools, and in the media. Children express the resulting pain of trauma in various ways, namely pain-based behaviors, which may manifest in everything from hyperarousal to dissociation. Not only can trauma affect a child's behavior patterns, but it also can actually permanently alter brain development. Trauma can occur not only when something is inflicted on a child, but also when something important is taken away. Children feel the effects of both tangible loss—something physical—and intangible loss—something emotional or psychological.

For the residential environment to be therapeutic, it must be a safe place where children feel comfortable letting down their guards. Workers can help create a culture of nonviolence by establishing structure and consistency, a secure base, discussing rules and limits in advance, avoiding stressful activities, and providing future-oriented activities. Workers must also be able to identify children's pain-based behaviors and respond in an appropriate and helpful manner. Workers should listen to children talk about their feelings, watch for triggers and signs of re-enactments and flashbacks to traumatic events, give children choices and control over life events, and teach children to better express and deal with their emotions. Though dealing with pain-based behavior may be difficult, annoying, or even scary, workers must remember that the behaviors they are seeing come from the child's painful past. Children need the help of those more experienced in dealing with emotions in order to learn how to cope better with their feelings. ✿

Self-Understanding and Emotional Competence

CHAPTER 10

First, Know Thyself

We don't see things as they are, we see them as we are.
—Anaïs Nin

Knowing oneself is basic to being a competent care worker. Part of the job of being a skilled and capable care worker is to identify and understand personal strengths, weaknesses, and values and to act on that self-assessment. Another important aspect of being a professional helper is taking care of one's own needs. Adults working with traumatized children are at risk of secondary trauma and need to have strategies to cope with the stress.

Everyone believes that they know how to parent children and what is best for the children in their care. Thousands of children in foster, group, and residential care can argue the validity of that belief. Everyone has a natural style and some skills when it comes to helping others, but this is not enough to help all of the children in care. Professional and effective care workers will develop a blend of their own natural abilities and learned concepts and skills. No matter how effective or skilled professional care workers are, there are always areas for improvement. Being able to assess one's own practice and work to improve skills are basic tenets of reflective practice.

Values and Personal Culture

Values are central to culture but are also developed by organizations, families, and individuals. Everyone has acquired their own set of beliefs and values through personal experiences and interactions with others. Over a lifetime, people develop assumptions and beliefs about themselves, other people, and the world in general. Values become principles that are cherished. These sets of assumptions, beliefs, and principles are used to make decisions and are what drives a person's behavior. For care workers, it is one thing to learn skills about working with children and young people; it is another thing to use the skills. A care worker's values will determine how or if the skills are used.

Ethnic and Multicultural Competence

The culture of others should be regarded as fundamental to their identity. When working with children, it is important to include their families to provide a link between development, behavior, and social orientation (Owusu-Bempah & Howitt, 2002). Children are best served when they remain intimately connected to their families, as their family's cultural environment is the foundation for how they have experienced life. For care workers to effectively help children from different backgrounds, including race, class, ethnicity, religion, sexual orientation, and gender, they must strive to be culturally competent. Cultural competence is the ability to understand another group from that group's own perspective (Wells-Wilbon & McDowell, 2001). It is an acquired skill.

Cultural competence in residential care begins by understanding one's own world-view as well as the world-view of the child. Care workers must acknowledge and understand their own world-view and how it differs from the child's. World-view is the lens through which people experience and view the world (Wells-Wilbon & McDowell, 2001). One of the ways to develop cultural competence is to immerse oneself into the child's cultural and ethnic reality by observing, participating, or asking the child and family for information. Once the differences in world-views are acknowledged, the door is opened for shared decision-making and exchange of information. Once the cultural context is understood, the care worker then can adjust activities, expectations, and style of interacting to the cultural values and preferences of the children and families. Care workers need to be sensitive to cultural differences and value systems of the children's ethnic and cultural group and adapt skills in response to the differing family patterns and lifestyles. Instead of assuming that interventions and treatment are generalized across all cultures, they need to be adapted to the unique needs of diverse children and families (Mohr et al., 2009).

Not acknowledging and accepting other's world-views can lead to racism and ethnocentrism. Assuming there is only one way to accomplish a task or reach a goal is ethnocentric and assumes that there is only one or a superior way of doing things that comes from the worker's world-view. For children who have had to deal with racism and powerlessness, this lack of understanding and acknowledgement leads to confusion, hostility, rage, and feeling devalued.

Self-Understanding and Emotional Competence

Understanding oneself and emotional competence are closely related (Goleman, 1998; Ivey & Ivey, 2003; Salovey, Mayer, &

Caruso, 2002). The five dimensions or domains that define emotional competence and are critical to working with children in care effectively are:

(1)   Self-awareness. Being aware of personal goals, values, beliefs about self and others; the rules by which one lives (the shoulds, musts, oughts); and self-talk, that inner voice that says do it or do not do it, are all part of self-awareness. All of these components come together to create personal views of the world and dictate behavior. When under pressure, as care workers often are, decisions are driven by one's world-view. Recognizing one's own emotions, strengths, limits, and values, contributes to making an accurate self-assessment and allows an individual to act with greater confidence and sense of purpose.

(2)   Self-motivation. Taking the initiative to develop new skills and abilities and achieving goals that in turn generate a feeling of self-confidence is self-motivation. Understanding a concept is not mastering a skill. Care workers who are self-motivated strive to develop new skills and seek out new information to improve their practice. Self-motivation also can be seen as the competent care worker's drive to meet a personal standard of excellence.

(3)   Empathy. The abilities to be empathic and to use good listening skills are closely related. Understanding people from different backgrounds, cultures, races, and ethnic groups and seeing their perspective is part of being empathic. The other part is the ability to communicate that understanding. This is a skill that will be discussed in greater detail later.

(4)   Social skills. As has been mentioned, relationship is central to helping children in care. Being able to establish trust, rapport, and confidence with the children and young people is necessary in order to be effective as a care worker. Being able to model social competence is essential if care workers are to help children become socially competent.

(5)   Self-regulation. As stated previously, this is the ability to manage emotions, a skill as important for the care worker as it is for the child. Knowing personal triggers, keeping emotions under control, showing flexibility to adapt to situations as they change, and maintaining standards of honesty and integrity are essential skills when working with emotionally troubled youth.

Secondary Trauma

Adults working with traumatized youth are at risk of secondary trauma. The symptoms of secondary trauma are less severe than those of primary trauma, but can affect the lives of care workers. Adults may feel overwhelmed, numb, shell-shocked, hopeless, or full of despair. They may feel unsafe. In some cases, counter-transference may occur when a young person's traumatic experience reminds the staff member of a personal experience. Sometimes staff may begin to identify with the young person resulting in the staff member's attempt to rescue the young person. Staff members become over-involved or try to prevent further suffering that interferes with the young person's ability to learn to cope with problems without assistance. At the other extreme, staff may withdraw from or avoid the young person, or minimize the young person's experiences in order to protect themselves. Secondary trauma can have a profound effect on the staff member's mental and physical health, as well as, professional performance.

Counteraggression

Everyone has had some traumatic or unpleasant events in their lives. A young person's behavior may be a reminder of being caught in a situation with an aggressive teacher, parent, or relative. This may trigger feelings of fear or vulnerabilities and counteraggression may be used as a protective response. Being aware of one's own personal triggers and vulnerabilities is an important part of being a competent care worker. If staff members are not in touch with their own feelings and triggers, staff may become counteraggressive in response to unpleasant and challenging behavior. Staff may feel out of control and may attempt to enforce stricter controls that only increase stress and pressure on the young person and themselves (Abramovitz & Bloom, 2003). Unfortunately the more staff members try to gain power and control through aggressive maneuvers, the more aggressive the young people become. It is a vicious cycle that must be avoided if a nonviolent culture is to be maintained.

There are many underlying reasons that staff may become counter aggressive, including responding to reminders of past traumatic events; reacting when children behave in a way that violates personal values and beliefs; and feeling helpless, rejected, or frustrated at one's own inability to help a child (Long, 1995). Counteraggressive behavior undermines staff effectiveness and the nonviolent culture of an organization. It reinforces children's beliefs that adults are hostile, hurtful, and rejecting. Preventing and controlling counteraggressive behaviors are difficult but critical skills for care workers.

Strategies for Coping with the Effects of Secondary Trauma

There are many ways adults can work to avoid or cope with the feelings they experience when working with traumatized children and young people. Organizations need to build in support systems and encourage all staff members to monitor their own levels of stress, take advantage of the support systems, and maintain a healthy lifestyle (Anglin, 2002; Fulcher & Ainsworth, 2006; Garfat, 2004; Krueger, 2007; Maier, 1987). Strategies include:

Have regular supervision at work. Using supervision effectively is a hallmark of a professional. Care workers should expect and participate in regular supervision that adheres to reflective practice principles. "How can I improve my skills and abilities in this work?" and "How can I keep my professional perspective?" are important questions to be discussed during supervision.

Develop an open and supportive, trauma-sensitive environment at work that includes regular discussion on secondary trauma. To avoid secondary trauma effects, everyone should feel free to acknowledge its existence. A culture of nonviolence helps prevent retraumatization as well as secondary trauma.

Maintain boundaries between personal and professional activities. Everyone needs down time—time to get away from the stress at work and enjoy personal relationships, hobbies, and family.

Engage in regular personal self-care activities such as exercise, hobbies, and social activities. The healthier the body and mind, the more resilient the care worker is when working with the stress and pain of the children in care. ✿

CHAPTER 11

Reflective Practice and Supervision

Reflective practice is a way of being in the world, a commitment as opposed to something a practitioner does.

— *Jo Trelfa*

Reflective practice is a process whereby individuals critically reflect on their own experiences and apply the knowledge gained from this introspection to improving their professional practice. This is done in conjunction with supervision and requires being coached by professionals in their field (Schon, 1996). This practice may be conducted by individuals or in groups.

Residential Care Workers and Reflective Practice

For residential care workers, reflective practice means continuously examining their own assumptions and practices in comparison to empirically proven best practice principles and strategies. It is an active process of observing one's own experience and analyzing it. The key to reflective practice is learning how to take perspective on one's own actions and experience—in other words, to examine the experience rather than just live it. The insight gained from self-reflection can open up great possibilities for increased effectiveness in the milieu.

The experiences that seem to provide the greatest opportunity for learning through reflective practice are those that contain elements of struggles, dilemmas, uncertainties, or breakthroughs (Amulya, 2004). By reflecting on action (looking back and deconstructing the situation), insight on one's own influence on the outcome of the situation may be gained. Reflective practice increases the possibility of learning from one's own work. For example, after an interaction with a child that resulted in the child's refusing to follow instructions and running out of the room, the care worker meets with the supervisor and deconstructs the event. What techniques and strategies did the worker use that increased the stress level of the child and what was used that decreased the stress level?

Practicing Reflection

Adhering to reflective practice principles means establishing a way to regularly examine one's own experiences through developing a habit, a structure, or a routine that allows time for the reflection. For optimum learning, it should be practiced frequently and based on a variety of experiences, both good and not so good. Following this reflection, the knowledge is used to improve skills. Workers can schedule reflection time individually and use supervision to practice reflection.

Practicing Reflection Collectively

Individual and collective reflection need not be mutually exclusive, that is, they can be accomplished together. Reflective practice "illuminates what the self and others have experienced" (Amulya, 2004). Since working as a team is a critical aspect of residential care, collectively using reflective practice principles is a way to improve collaborative interventions (Ruch, 2005, 2007). Reflecting individually and with colleagues can be a supportive and learning experience. For example, an event with a child involving several staff members, both directly and indirectly, would be a good opportunity for reflection individually and collectively. In collectively reflecting on the incident, each individual could take a turn recounting the event and then getting feedback, analyzing, making connections, formulating critical questions, and learning from the experience.

Reflecting in Practice

In addition to reflecting on one's experience and learning from it, care workers can reflect in practice or as events are occurring. As workers gain skills at examining their own actions, there may be moments during interactions with children when workers can examine what they are doing as they are doing it. If it is not working, the worker can adjust his or her approach immediately and reflect on its effectiveness. Through the process of ongoing reflections both individually and collectively, and practicing reflectively, more effective child and youth care practice emerges to the benefit of the children and the organization.

Summary

Children in care come from a variety of ethnic and cultural backgrounds. For workers to be able to provide an environment accepting of everyone, they must be both knowledgeable and accepting of other cultures and their practices, as well as being aware of their own background, strengths, and weaknesses. Also important to a worker's self-awareness is emotional competence, which encompasses self-awareness, self-regulation, self-motivation, empathy, and social skills. Being aware of one's own actions and views and how one is affecting others is key when working with children who look at care workers as role models. Workers must also be wary of the effects of secondary trauma, or, the effects of a child's trauma on their own actions and thinking. Having regular supervision, participating in open discussions on the effects of secondary trauma, maintaining personal boundaries, and engaging in self-care activities can assist workers in avoiding the negative effects of secondary trauma.

Reflective practice enables workers to learn through their own experience by examining their own practice individually and in supervision. By comparing actions to best practice standards and by examining the consequences of how situations were handled, workers can improve their skills and become more competent. Workers should be honest with themselves about their actions and examine not only the things they have done right, but also what has gone wrong. When reflective practice is done collectively, workers get a chance to learn not only from their own experiences, but also from those of others. In this way, knowledge and experience can be maximized and care standards will become closer to best practice. ✿

CREATING CONDITIONS FOR CHANGE

CHAPTER 12

Supporting Behavior Change

Bitter are the tears of a child: Sweeten them.
Deep are the thoughts of a child: Quiet them.
Sharp is the grief of a child: Take it from him.
Soft is the heart of a child: Do not harden it.

—*Pamela Glenconner*

Children and adolescents come to residential care with a variety of life experiences and resultant ways of behaving and coping because of those experiences. In care, assistance is deployed to help young people cope with loss and trauma and heal their pain and hurt. By providing a therapeutic milieu and protective factors which include adults with the skills and capacity to form healthy attachments; routines that satisfy basic needs; opportunities for normal developmental activities; and a nonviolent atmosphere that promotes physical and emotional safety, children are able to progress along normal developmental pathways. Their innate capacity to form relationships and learn new skills is freed up (Benard, 2004). This is slow, incremental change that takes place as children practice new skills and experience satisfying results from their efforts. Henry Maier called this developmental type of change, first order change (Maier, 1987, p. 17).

In residential care, children and adolescents not only are expected to achieve normal developmental tasks and learn new skills, but to learn to behave, think, and feel differently, which is second order change. Producing second order change (Maier, 1987, p. 17) is an additional expectation for providers of residential care and treatment. Children must unlearn some behaviors that are destructive and learn new, more adaptive skills, learn how to think, feel, and act differently. To assist children in this endeavor, care workers must have greater skill, more flexibility, and carry out substantial interventions that produce more than normal developmental growth. Care workers must help children heal old wounds and then teach them how to live differently. The task is to assist the children in developing skills and competencies to improve their quality of life. Care workers cannot just be good at parenting and caring for children, they must consciously make decisions about how to interact, intervene, teach, lead, encourage, and communicate based on the specific needs of the child at that specific time, in that specific environment.

Making Changes

Changing a pattern of behavior is never easy. Once considered, people will struggle to change a personal habit or behavior they have found dissatisfying. They may try several ways to quit smoking, start exercising, stop complaining, control their temper, and so on, before they are successful. What helps people change behavior? How can care workers help children change? Changing one's own behavior is complicated enough; helping someone else change is even more complex.

There are specific factors that contribute to any person's ability to change behaviors. The most important one is what the person brings to the process (Lambert, 1992). (See Table 1. Factors That Affect Change In Children.) The child's personal strengths, resources, beliefs, and life experiences provide approximately 40% of the contribution toward change. The second most significant factor, about 30%, is the relationship between the child and the adult (Benard, 2004; Holmqvist, Hill, & Lang, 2007; Hubble et al., 1999; Lovett, 1996; Maier, 1987; Trieschman et al., 1969). Does the child perceive the relationship as an alliance based on empathy, acceptance, understanding, warmth, and encouragement?

Another factor that adds to the success of the change process is the child's and the worker's expectation and hopefulness about the change (Benard, 2004; de Schipper, Riksen-Walraven, Geurts, & Derksen, 2008; Garbarino, 1999; Hubble et al., 1999). Does the child believe he or she can change? If the child takes the risk and tries a new behavior, does he or she believe it will work? Is the child hopeful? Does the care worker communicate hopefulness and a belief in the ability of the child to change? Does the worker have high expectations for the child? Although this only

TABLE 1. Factors That Affect Change In Children

Factors that Influence Change in Children	% Effect on Change
The child's personal strengths, resources, beliefs, and life experiences	40%
The relationship between the child and the adult	30%
The child's own and the worker's expectations and hopefulness about the change	15%
The actual technique or intervention used to facilitate the change	15%

Note: Although the actual percentages shown here are based on Michael Lambert's (1992) research on what accounted for improvement in clients in therapy, the same elements have been identified throughout the literature (Garbarino, 1999; Hubble, 1995; Lovett, 1996; Maier,1987; Trieschman et al., 1969) as having significant impact on children's behavioral change.

contributes 15% to the change process, it certainly has an impact. The last factor (15%) is the actual technique or model used to facilitate the change (Holmqvist et al., 2007; Hubble et al., 1999). What is the therapeutic orientation used by the care worker and organization? What are the beliefs about how children change? What strategies are the care workers using to influence children's behavior?

Helping Children Change Their Behavior

A primary reason children are placed in care is for professionals to assist them in changing their behaviors. Essentially care workers are tasked with helping children stop or decrease inappropriate, destructive, deviant, dangerous behaviors and replace them with adaptive, age-appropriate, productive behaviors. This becomes a dual mission of meeting a child's needs and helping the child develop new competencies to deal with life's situations. A care worker gives to the child (meets the child's needs) and expects something from the child (learn new skills). To be effective at teaching alternative behaviors, care workers need to know exactly what the undesirable behavior is, when it occurs, who it is directed toward, what the intent of the behavior is, and what it means developmentally. Before attempting to substitute alternative behaviors, understanding the *what, when, who, and why* of the behavior is necessary. Then the behavior needs to be interrupted and a substitute behavior taught. There are potential ethical issues when one person is trying to change another person's behavior, especially when it is an adult working with a child. There is an inherent and unavoidable balance of power. It is important to practice ethically and act humanely. The care worker's role is one of healer and teacher. ✿

CHAPTER *13*

Discovering the Child's Potential

If I have the belief that I can do it, I shall surely acquire the capacity to do it even if I may not have it at the beginning.

—*Mahatma Gandhi*

The child's life experiences are a major part of what the child brings to the change process. As discussed previously, these life experiences may be filled with hurt, failure, deprivation, and pain. The care worker's role is to assist the child in identifying the strengths and assets he or she has and to instill hope that things can change. To assist children in developing new pro-social behaviors, it is important to help children identify the resources that they bring to the cause. This may be a difficult task since most children arrive in care with a list of deficits and problems. The focus has been on the negative behaviors.

As discussed previously, the tendency in residential care (sometimes to justify placement) is to describe children in terms of what they are not doing or what they are doing poorly. It may take a major readjustment in the eyes and minds of both staff and the young people to change the conversation to what they are doing and what they do well. If the focus is on the strengths and positive attributes of the young person, not only does the path to change become more apparent and achievable, the young person may start developing a positive identity (a major task of adolescence).

Strategies for change are more effective if they are targeted at the child's current level of operation or zone of proximal development and build on the child's strengths. Care workers can then create the optimum conditions for the child to use those strengths in testing out the desired behaviors. By identifying the positive attributes the child brings to the change process and building on those, the chance of positive change is increased.

Able, Willing, and Ready

The strengths have been identified, and the behavior to be changed has been described as to when, where, who, and why. The care worker has tailored the environment so that the child has a better chance at success and nothing happens. The child does not make the effort. What is missing?

Before someone is ready to change, they must be willing and able. Being able means having the necessary knowledge, skills, and resources to move forward—what the child brings to the change process. Being willing is more complicated; it involves courage, trust, and belief. Being ready to change means that the child believes that he or she can succeed and can hope for a different future. The child's expectations of him or herself are also important factors in changing behavior. The belief that one has about his or her own ability to accomplish a task is called self-efficacy and is a critical factor in someone's willingness to take on a challenge (Bandura, 1994).

Great Expectations

The children's expectations of themselves (self-efficacy) influence their willingness to put forth effort to cope with life's difficulties, overcome obstacles, and change behaviors. Four components contribute to shaping a person's self-efficacy (Bandura, 1994, 1997; Pajares & Urdan, 2006). Working within these areas can help care workers motivate and inspire children to take risks and try new behaviors.

(1)   Experience. To shape children's belief about what they can achieve—their self-efficacy—they must have experiences that are successful. They must have proof that they can master the task. This is the most influential component of increasing one's self-efficacy and is part of an ecological perspective; people are shaped by their interactions with their environment.

(2)   Modeling. Seeing peers and people like themselves succeed can bolster self-efficacy. Children compare themselves against their peers, a part of normal development, and if their peers can succeed, it gives them confidence. On the other hand, if their peers fail it decreases their self-efficacy.

(3)   Social persuasion. A word of encouragement from the right person at the right time can have a major influence in altering a child's confidence. Unfortunately, negative persuasion is easier and more powerful. It is easier to decrease someone's self-efficacy than to increase it. This is an important point for care workers in monitoring what they say and what others say to the children in their care. Children are easily defeated by words.

(4)   Physiological and emotional factors. The amount of stress, fear, or nervousness can alter a person's willingness to try something. Again, it is not necessarily just having these physical and emotional responses—it is how the person perceives them that is important. Getting anxious and queasy before making a presentation might give some folks the "edge" they need to do well. Other people may take it as a sign that they cannot possibly get up in front of people and speak. It may immobilize them.

Strengthening Self-Efficacy

It is important to work toward increasing the child's sense of self-efficacy (Egan, 2002). Improving a child's self-efficacy can increase the child's ability and willingness to change. There are several strategies available that care workers can use in this endeavor.

Give help with skill development. Before challenging a child to try a new behavior, it is critical that the child has the necessary skills and a sense of competence to use them. It is more than being able to do something, it is the confidence that the skill is going to work and will accomplish the goal. Anyone who has learned a new skill in a training program has had to overcome the *feeling incompetent in using the skill* stage in order to move to the *this skill will work for me and improve my performance* stage. Everyone has skills they can demonstrate, but do not use in practice. Helping someone develop skills and the confidence to use them requires several steps.

(1) Teach skills and allow for plenty of graduated practice experiences. Assess what skills are needed for the alternative behavior, teach the skill(s), practice the skill(s) in easy, non-challenging situations, and then gradually practice the skill realistically in a variety of situations.

(2) Give corrective feedback on the child's performance, not the child's personality, in a way that increases the child's sense of efficacy. *Yesterday in the community meeting, you sat quietly and listened to everyone's ideas, which is what we have* *been practicing. Let me make a suggestion. You do not have to be totally silent. You can listen to other's ideas and suggest ideas that you like.* Also give specific, positive feedback to emphasize the child's strengths and reinforce the child's use of the new skill(s). *During the community meeting today, you offered an idea of your own after listening to other ideas. The other boys felt listened to and could also hear your idea, which several boys also liked. You contributed to the group.*

(3)   **Create the conditions for positive results.** Success often provides the momentum to try again and try harder. The child who succeeds at a task will more likely have the courage to try again and under more difficult circumstances. Allow the child to try out the new behavior in situations where he or she can succeed. It is the care worker's job to make sure the child succeeds.

   Point out successful models. Children and adolescents use peers as a reference group. Younger children measure their own competency by comparing themselves to other children. Adolescents establish an identity and separate from adults by interacting with and relating to their peer group. When children and adolescents see their peers succeed, they are encouraged to try. *If he can do it, so can I.* In residential care, it is important to have children with a variety of strengths in a group, so that they can provide positive models for each other.

   Provide encouragement and support. This has to be genuine and tailored to the individual. The support and encouragement should be targeted to something real. It is more than, *Come on, you can do it,* which can easily be interpreted as condescending. Encouraging someone to find a situation that feels safe enough to try out a new skill and providing the support the person needs to attempt it, is what will improve self-efficacy.

Reduce the child's fears. If a child is afraid of failing, he or she is not likely to try. Helping children find ways to reduce their fears and anxieties about the new challenge will heighten their self-efficacy and willingness to act. Relaxation exercises, talking about their fears with others, and pointing out past successes are all ways to help reduce fears and anxieties.

All of these strategies will assist the children to have faith in their abilities to accomplish tasks and be successful in their attempts. It will help the children believe that the future could be different—better for them. It is the adult's responsibility to help each child have a great day, every day. The care workers are not only hoping the child will succeed, but orchestrating each attempt so that it will be successful. ✿

CHAPTER 14

The Relationship As a Therapeutic Alliance

The greatest compliment that was ever paid me was when one asked me what I thought, and attended to my answer.

—Henry David Thoreau

The importance of building attachments so children have a secure base to feel safe, grow, and develop is a primary learning point in this book. The attachment relationship provides the platform for *first-order* change as it paves the way for the child to have a secure base to progress along normal developmental pathways. This primary relationship developed by providing attachment-building experiences for the child, is a necessary building block for *second-order* change. When children are asked to change their coping behaviors—those very behaviors which have protected them and helped them deal with painful feelings and traumatic events—they are being asked to take huge risks. As mentioned previously, a therapeutic relationship or alliance based on empathy, acceptance, understanding, warmth, and encouragement is the second most significant factor in the change process. A therapeutic alliance with a trusted adult can make the change process less frightening and more manageable.

The word alliance infers a partnership. Within this framework, helping a child does not mean doing something to the child, but rather means working with the child to accomplish mutually agreed goals. It means being in the relationship and being *real* in the relationship. The relationship becomes the therapeutic alliance through which change is facilitated.

Building the Relationship

Real behavior change is facilitated through relationships. The more serious the need for change, the more significant the relationship needs to be. Relationships are interactions between people. They are established through the personal experiences that people have with each other over time. A key question to ask in evaluating the quality of the relationship between the child and care worker is, "Does the child perceive the relationship as an alliance based on empathy, acceptance, respect, understanding, warmth, and encouragement?" Four fundamental factors were previously identified as necessary in helping children form positive attachments to adults. These were availability, sensitivity, acceptance, and investment. These qualities are the basis for the child to attach positively and establish trust with the adult. Where does the relationship go from there? Therapeutic alliances are comprised of several additional characteristics, including trust, empathy, validation, respect, and genuineness (Anglin, 2002; Benard, 2004; Brendtro, 2004; Brendtro & Ness, 1983; Egan, 2002; de Schipper et al., 2008; Hardy & Laszloffy, 2005; Holmqvist et al., 2007; Hubble et al., 1999; Krueger, Glaovits, Wilder, & Pick; 1999; Laursen & Birmingham, 2003; Lovett, 1996; Maier, 1991).

Trust Is the Foundation

Trust is relying on someone and is the basis for caring relationships. The establishment of trust begins with a positive attachment experience. There is no shortcut in establishing trust in a relationship. Trust is built on the experience that two people share with each other. The care worker must be trustworthy by following words with actions. By being dependable, consistent, and available, the care worker earns a child's trust.

To earn trust, trust must also be extended. Trust is a two-way process (Brendtro & Ness, 1983; Egan, 2002). The care worker must extend trust to the child in realistic doses. The child needs to trust the adult to create the conditions for the child to succeed. The adult must trust the child to do as well as he or she can in the situation. Care workers who are focused on building trusting relationships never ask children to do something that they cannot do. For the child to take risks and develop skills, the child needs to trust that the care worker would never ask him or her to do something that he or she is not capable of doing.

Empathy—Walking in Their Shoes

Empathy is seeing the world though another's eyes or, as is commonly said, *walking in another person's shoes*. Being empathic with a child means accurately understanding and feeling what the child feels from his or her orientation or point of reference and communicating that understanding to the child (Brendtro & Ness, 1983; Egan, 2002; Hubble et al., 1999; Hutchens & Vaught, 1997). It requires being sensitive to what is going on with another person and understanding the person's experience, point of view, and world view. A care worker must be able to attend, observe, and listen to the child in order to get inside the child's world and experience it as the child does. It requires listening to the child's stories and listening for the feelings, emotions, and moods of the child. As the child speaks, the worker listens for the child's point of view, how the child sees the future, and what values, goals, and perspectives the child has.

The other half of empathy is communicating the understanding back to the child. The care worker must be able to listen empathically and communicate that understanding to the child. "You feel bad, not because you can't go tonight, but because he broke his promise."

Validation Affirms Self-Worth

Validation is acknowledging someone's strengths and perspective. Affirming and validating is sending the message that the child's perspective is understood—*I see where you are coming from, I understand.* It does not mean agreement; it is acknowledgement. It is treating someone with positive regard and instilling self-worth (Brendtro, 2004; Hardy & Laszloffy, 2005). Care workers can validate a child's feelings, goals, and world view by listening and acknowledging that they hear and understand the child's perspective.

Respect

Respect is showing consideration and treating the young person as a person with value. Respect is such a common term it almost defies definition. Being respectful includes showing proper acceptance, courtesy, and acknowledgement for the child's family, culture, race, and life experiences. Everyone inherently knows what it feels like to be respected and what it feels like to be disrespected. Disrespect looms big in the complaints of children in care. Some young people are willing to go to extremes, even give up their lives, to gain respect and maintain their dignity. Being respectful includes listening, giving choices, and taking their viewpoint into consideration. The Golden Rule applies here (for example, *Do unto others as you would have them do unto you.*).

Genuineness Is Being Real

Genuineness is being congruent and real, knowing oneself and representing oneself honestly—*What you see is what you get.* This means being honest and avoiding fakery or false platitudes. Children quickly detect when an adult is being condescending or covering up his or her own feelings (Egan, 2002; Hardy & Laszloffy, 2005). Being genuine entails speaking to children person-to-person, not talking down to them.

The Power of the Relationship

Once the relationship is established, the care worker's influence is more powerful within the change process (Maier, 1991; Trieschman et al., 1969). It is important to put the relationship first, nurture the relationship and have fun together. With the therapeutic alliance in place, the child is more likely to communicate with the adult, providing valuable information that will help the care worker respond to the needs of the child. Children take suggestions and directions more readily from someone they trust and who trusts them. The care worker's influence is greatly increased as the child wishes to maintain the relationship and please the adult, providing powerful social control. Control is embedded within the relationship.

Finally, the relationship enhances the care worker's role as a model for the child. The care worker's opinion matters to the child. Children will imitate people they admire and respect and with whom they have a relationship. Caring and trusting relationships protect children from risk, help them overcome trauma, and boost their resiliency.

Establishing Personal Boundaries

Being in a relationship is a personal experience through which insight into one's own values, beliefs, and emotions are exposed. Care workers need to acknowledge that if they are to be effective in this work and build relationships with children and young people, they will need to be committed to personal and professional growth and development (Fewster, 1990; Krueger, 2007; Ruch, 2007). Through reflective practice, care workers can stay aware of any personal "baggage" that may be influencing their responses to children. Care workers must expect children to throw up barriers and roadblocks in the relationship. What one experiences in one particular relationship should not carry over to other relationships. Keeping things clear between relationships is important. Establishing boundaries within the relationships with the children is an ongoing process and must meet the needs of the child, the care worker, and the organization.

Summary

Many factors affect a child's ability to change, including the child's own strengths (40%), the relationship between the child and the adult assisting them in change (30%), hopefulness about the change (15%), and the actual technique used to change (15%). Children in care are often there because of inappropriate and maladaptive behavior patterns. One of the main tasks of care workers is to help children find new ways of behaving that will serve them better both in the present environment and in the future.

It is important for workers to see the child's potential and have faith in each child and in the child's ability to change. For someone to change, they must be able, willing, and ready—if any one of these elements is missing, change will be nearly impossible.

Part of a child being ready to change is the child's self-efficacy, or belief in self, which is shaped by experiences, modeling by peers, social persuasion, and psychological and emotional factors. Several strategies are useful to strengthen a child's self-efficacy, including helping with skill development, providing successful models with which the child can identify, providing encouragement and support, and reducing the child's fear about failure.

A care worker's relationship with a child is a unique and powerful tool to use when helping a child to change maladaptive behaviors. Key characteristics of strong relationships include trust, empathy, validation, respect, and genuineness. With these ingredients, a strong relationship between child and worker can be forged; one that will influence both parties in a positive way. ✿

HELPING CHILDREN DO WELL

CHAPTER *15*

Teaching Self-Regulation Skills

Children do well if they can. If they can't, we need to figure out why so we can help.

—*Ross Greene*

What happens when children fail to meet expectations? Break the rules? Refuse to comply with requests? Use inappropriate behaviors to meet their needs or communicate their distress? Asking this question of a group of care workers would probably elicit a variety of responses. Some workers might say, "Hold them accountable!" or "Give them consequences!" Others might advise, "Discipline them!" or even "Punish them." The manner in which a child's pain-based behavior is responded to is one of the key indicators of the quality of care as experienced by the children (Anglin, 2002; Brendtro & Shahbazian, 2004). How can care workers choose the best response at the right time to maintain the program, keep everyone safe and secure, enhance relationships, teach children self-regulation skills, and increase the child's self-efficacy?

The first thing to consider when a child fails to meet the expectation is where the focus should be. How important is it for the child to meet the expectation and/or follow the rule? If the expectations and rules are important for teaching pro-social skills, maintaining the functioning of the group, enhancing relationship skills, and/or keeping children and staff safe, then the focus should be on those expectations or rules, not on the violation. The question then becomes, *What does the child need in order to meet the expectation or follow the rule?* The answer lies in the assessment of what it is the child lacks at that moment to succeed. Does the child understand what is required? Does the child have the skills necessary to meet the expectation? Can the child control his or her emotions at the moment? Is the child motivated to meet the expectation? Does it make sense for this child given the child's world-view?

There are two decisions for the care worker to make in the moment: (1) How important is it for the child to meet the expectation at this moment? (2) What does the child need to succeed?

Observe and Assess, Then Respond

The ears and the eyes are closer to the brain than the mouth. This can help remind adults that it is important to observe how the child looks and what the child is doing, listen to what the child is saying, decide what the child needs at that moment to meet the expectation, and then speak. When a child is not meeting expectations, assess the situation.

Example: The care worker walks in the room at chore time and Johnnie is pacing around the room while the rest of the children are doing their chores.

(1) **Observe: Look and listen.** A care worker needs to be able to read each child's rhythm through body language and verbal and nonverbal behaviors in order to provide the support and encouragement that the individual child needs to manage daily activities. It is important to pay attention to what children are doing instead of what they are not doing. Observing how the child is behaving gives much more valuable information than deciding why the child is doing or not doing something. Observe what the child is doing. Listen to what the child is saying. What is the function of the behavior? Observe how the child looks. Is the child in distress, having a stress response? Afraid, angry, calm?

Example: Johnnie is pacing around the room. He looks upset and agitated. Pacing seems to be the way he is dealing with his anxiety.

(2) Assess: Take a moment to think. Once the care worker has noted how the child is behaving, it is time to put that behavior in context and/or the framework for understanding. Is this behavior normal for this child at this time of day during this activity? Is this behavior an attempt to express a feeling, gain control over a situation, or try out new skills? Assess what the child needs in order to meet expectations and if it is necessary to meet the expectation at this moment. Does the child need to relax, calm down? Does the adult need to calm down? Does the child understand the expectation? Does the child understand why it is important? What is the message he is trying to communicate? Does the child have the skills (intellectual and emotional) to meet the expectation? All of these questions are ones that care workers can ask themselves each day in order to understand the actions and feelings of the children in their care. Being sensitive to what is going on with the child is important in determining how to respond.

Example: Johnnie is easily upset and has a hard time attending when agitated. He may not be able to respond to a request. Johnnie does understand that it is chore time and he has been able to do his chores all week.

(3) Respond. Based on observations and assessment of the situation, various responses may be called on if the children are struggling to manage routines and meet expectations. It is important to choose a response that meets the child's needs at that moment and helps the child meet the expectation. Pick a response that will calm, explain, teach, or motivate depending on the assessment. Decide how important the expectation is versus what the child needs at the moment.

Example: What will help Johnnie meet the expectation of doing his chores? How important is it for Johnnie to do the chores at this moment?

Choosing a Response

Effective interventions between care workers and children facilitate behavior change, teach self-regulation skills, enhance relationships, decrease the child's pain and stress, de-escalate the behavior, avoid power struggles, and teach effective coping skills (Gardner et al., 2008; Gestsdottir & Lerner, 2008; Gibson, 2005; Greene, 2001; Greene & Ablon, 2006; Hardy & Laszloffy, 2005; Hawkin-Rodgers, 2007; M. J. Holden et al., 2009; Maier, 1991; Shiendling, 1995). There are five basic types of responses available for care workers to use (Greene, 2001; Greene & Ablon, 2006; Shiendling, 1995). The key is to pick the right approach, at the right time, in the right situation, and be flexible enough to switch the approach if the child's response is not what was desired.

Option: Acknowledge When the Child Is Meeting Expectations

It is often easier to see what the child is not doing or should not be doing rather than look for the child's strengths and reinforce what the child is doing well. To help children have high expectations and believe in themselves, care workers can change their focus to what the child is able to do and has accomplished.

When to acknowledge the positive behavior. The first step in deciding to acknowledge the child's behavior is to observe what the child is doing. If the child is successfully accomplishing the expectation or part of the expectation, the assessment would be that the expectation is reasonable and appropriate and that the child is able (has the skills, knowledge, and resources) and willing (has the courage, trust, and belief) to meet it. The response is to acknowledge and reinforce the child's ability and willingness to achieve. This is now one of the child's strengths to be built upon. The result is that the expectation is met and the child's self-efficacy is strengthened by the successful experience. (See Table 2.)

Response techniques that acknowledge behavior. There are many ways to respond positively to children's behavior. These

---

Table 2. Acknowledge When the Child Is Meeting Expectations

Observe
▼
Child is doing laundry

Assess
▼
Child is willing
Child is able
Expectation is reasonable

Response
▼
Acknowledge the child's behavior

Result
▼
Child's self-efficacy increases
Therapeutic alliance is strengthened
Expectation is met

---

range from acknowledging children's strengths and abilities to using built-in programmatic responses. Some examples follow:

(1)   Give positive attention. Simply tell the child that you think that the child has done a good job.

Example: "Johnnie, you did a good job washing the dishes today. Thank you."

(2)   Join in the activity. As the child begins the stated task, the care worker joins the child to emphasize the importance of the expectations.

Example: "Let me help with some of the dishes, there are a lot of them and it is important that we get them done."

(3)   Ask the child to teach others. Recognize the child's accomplishment by asking the child to assist someone else.

Example: "Johnnie, you have done a good job with the dishes, could you show Eddie how you do them since it will be his job next week?"

Option: Encourage the Child To Meet the Expectation

As discussed previously, rules, routines, and expectations should be discussed, understood, and agreed upon in advance of problem situations. It is essential that care workers, as part of their everyday interactions and activities, are working with the children to help them develop the skills necessary to meet expectations and follow the routines and rules before using intervention strategies that focus on the expectation. When children are not meeting expectations and the care worker has assessed that all the child needs is a little push in the right direction, using encouragement and explaining the expectation may be all that is necessary (Greene, 2001; Greene & Ablon, 2006; Shiendling, 1995). This approach helps maintain the program and assists children in meeting expectations.

When To Use Encouragement

Before using an approach that encourages the child to meet the expectation, certain criteria should be met (Greene, 2001; Greene & Ablon, 2006).

(1)   The expectation is important enough to risk escalating the situation.

(2)   The child has demonstrated the ability to meet the expectation on a regular basis.

(3)   The child is calm enough to attend to and respond to the request. (See Table 3.)

Table 3. Encourage the Child To Meet the Expectation

Observe

Child is not doing laundry

Assess

Child is able
Child is not willing
Expectation is reasonable

Response

Encourage
Explain

Result

Child's self-efficacy is maintained
Therapeutic alliance is strengthened
Expectation is met

Response Techniques That Encourage Children To Meet Expectations

There are several ways a care worker can respond to help children meet expectations and follow the routine (M. J. Holden et al., 2009; Maier, 1991; Redl & Wineman, 1952). It is best to start with gentle reminders and requests before making stronger demands.

As if. Sometimes, the child simply needs a reminder or prompt of what the expectation is. He or she may be momentarily distracted or not quite ready to begin the task. In this case, a simple statement of the expectation and then continuing "as if" the child will achieve the goal (Maier, 1991) may be all that is necessary. Care workers should communicate routines, rules, and procedures with "expectation in their voice" (Anglin, 2002, p. 68). The care worker has the expectation that the child will succeed and acts as if it will be accomplished. Remind the child (without nagging) of the expectation. The care worker communicates through tone of voice and choice of words that he or she expects the young person to follow the routine and meet the expectation.

Example: Johnnie, it is time to do chores. What do you need to do your chore?

Offer assistance. Sometimes children and young people need a little help to get started or finish a task. When a trusted adult offers to help the child meet the expectation. It is often enough to get the child back on track. This not only helps children meet expectations, but helps build attachments and therapeutic alliances.

Example: Let me help you with your chore, I'll get the broom. If you wash the dishes, I'll dry them.

Give choices. There are times when the child may have conflicting priorities or opportunities to participate in competing activities. Although expectations and routines may be set, there are always many ways to meet those expectations. For example, the schedule may show it is time to do chores, but the child has the opportunity to participate in a recreational activity with a friend.

Working with the child to look at the schedule and make adjustments so that expectations can be met and the child can participate in the activity teaches children how to manage their time and responsibilities. If the child is struggling with the expectation at the moment, offer two or three attractive alternatives.

Example: You can do your chore now and I'll help you get started or you can take your free time now and do your chore during free time later.

Predict the future. Children can get stuck in the moment and need some help seeing that the task at hand can be accomplished and other more enjoyable activities follow. Care workers can remind the child of what happens in the future once the expectation is met. This may help the child be more willing to meet the expectation by anticipating a positive outcome.

Example: Once chores are finished, you can go outside and play ball. As soon as you finish with your chore, we can play a video game together.

Make a request. With a good relationship between the care worker and child, the adult can often motivate the child to meet the expectation by just asking for cooperation. Challenge the child to make a good decision.

Example: You know the routine. Johnnie, do your chores; let's have a good day. Johnnie, you know what you are doing isn't what is expected. Make a better choice.

This is an effective technique if the child is calm enough to honor the request. If a child is in a stress response mode (too upset), he or she may not be able to manage his or her emotions enough to respond to a request or make a good choice. In this case, the focus on the expectation will probably result in a power struggle or crisis situation. The stronger the request, the more the care worker is relying on his or her authority and relationship with the child, so the child must recognize the adult as an authority figure and someone the child wishes to please. If the child is too upset to manage the request (does not have good self-regulation skills), the care worker does not have a good relationship with the child, or the child does not recognize the worker's authority, the child may escalate. If the worker resorts to threats or touches the child, it may evoke a fear or stress response and the child may go into "fight" or "flight" mode.

Option: Change the Expectation

There may be times when the most important thing is to reduce the level of frustration. This can apply to an individual or a group of children. Sometimes the expectation can be changed or be forgotten altogether. This is useful when children do not have sufficient self-regulation skills to manage their emotions, are not meeting expectations and the care worker has assessed that the expectation is not that critical at this moment, or when the child cannot meet the expectation at this moment, and, if pursued, the situation will definitely escalate (Greene 2001; Greene & Ablon, 2006; M. J. Holden et al., 2009; Shiendling, 1995). This approach prevents crises and prioritizes the critical expectations that need to be met and/or taught now and those that can be dealt with later when the child is more likely to succeed.

When To Change the Expectation

Before changing the expectation, the following should be considered (Greene 2001; Greene & Ablon, 2006; Maier, 1991):

(1) There is reason to believe that the child is unable to succeed under the circumstances. It is an unrealistic expectation.

(2) There is no immediate danger in changing or dropping the expectation.

(3) By adjusting the expectation, the child will be able to succeed. (See Table 4)

TABLE 4. CHANGE THE EXPECTATION

Observe

Child is not doing laundry

Assess

Child is not able (lacks skills, knowledge, resources)
Child is not willing (lacks trust, belief, courage)
Expectation is not reasonable at this moment

Response

Redirect
Change expectation

Result

Child did not escalate (self-efficacy is maintained)
Therapeutic alliance is maintained
Expectation is not met or may be partially met

Response Techniques That Change the Expectation

The following techniques help care workers change, reduce, or drop expectations (Maier, 1991; Redl & Wineman, 1952).

Change the expectations. If the expectation is problematic for an individual or group, adapt it to something so that children can be successful.

Example: After school, you can take a 20 minute break and then do your chores. Instead of sweeping the floor today, why don't you do the dusting?

Redirect the activity. When the activity itself is causing the anxiety, change the activity.

Example: Let's all go take a walk. We can do chores later. Why don't we make some popcorn and talk about what is going on.

Drop the expectation. Take a holiday from the expectation or have someone else do it on the child's behalf.

Example: I am declaring today a holiday from chores. Let's go outside and play. You are really stressed out today, I'll sweep for you today and you can chill.

Adjusting or dropping expectations can be used with the group or the individual. It can also be used proactively. For example, if the child is too tired from a rough day and it is obvious that meeting expectations may overwhelm what resources the child has left, drop or reduce the expectation in advance. If the child has not been able to meet the expectations under any circumstances, change them so that the child can live successfully within the expectations. This approach is not seen as letting children *get away with something*, but as a way to keep children involved in the program and build their self-efficacy. A main priority for care workers is to assure that each child has a successful day.

Option: Teach the Child—Communicate and Problem-Solve

When the situation can be used to teach children how to manage their own emotions and behaviors, meet expectations, and solve problems, care workers can rely on a more collaborative approach. This approach assists children in meeting expectations by drawing on their strengths, valuing their input, respecting their worldview, and helping them develop life skills. This strategy should be used whenever possible as it accomplishes several tasks all at once. It helps the child meet expectations; maintains the integrity of the program; enhances the adult-child relationship; teaches children social competencies, cognitive skills, and how to manage their emotions and behaviors; and prevents future problems.

When to Teach the Child

It is best to use this technique (Greene, 2001; Greene & Ablon, 2006) when:

(1)   The care worker and child are both calm enough to discuss the problem about meeting expectations without escalating the situation.

(2)   There is reason to believe that the child does not have the necessary cognitive and/or emotional skills to meet the expectation consistently.

(3)   There is flexibility in how the expectation can be met (such as, there are a variety of ways to solve the problem and address all concerns). (See Table 5.)

Table 5. Teach the Child

Observe

Child is not doing laundry

Assess

Child is not able (lacks skills, knowledge, resources)
Child is willing
Expectation is reasonable or may need adjustment

Response

Communicate
Problem-solve
Teach

Result

Child learns new skills (self-efficacy is increased)
Therapeutic alliance is strengthened
Expectation is met

Response Techniques That Teach the Child

Care workers can use a problem-solving model to help children learn skills that they need in order to meet expectations and develop self-regulation skills (Greene, 2001; Greene & Ablon, 2006; Hardy & Laszloffy, 2005).

(1) Listen, validate, and respond with respect. The child may appear confused or upset. Sometimes children have a lot on their mind or are concerned about something that happened during the day. They are not concentrating on the task at hand and are having trouble focusing on the expectation. Sometimes listening and empathizing are what is needed. Empathic listening and open questions are the primary techniques used to find out what is keeping the child from meeting expectations. It is important to validate the child's strengths and perceptions. The care worker needs to not only understand what the child is feeling and thinking and trying to accomplish, but needs to communicate that understanding to the child.

Example: Johnnie, you appear to be upset, can you tell me what is bothering you?

I can see how stressed out you are right now, is it something about doing your chores or did something else happen to upset you?

When you came back from school today, you declared that you were not going to do chores. You are upset about failing a test at school. Is that why you are pacing?

(2) **Define the problem.** After the care worker has identified and validated the child's concern, it is time to define the problem clearly. What are the concerns that need to be addressed? Are these everyone's concerns?

Example: It is chore time, all of the children are busy doing their chores. You failed a test at school today and are too upset to sweep the floor. You need a break. My concern is that if you take a break, you will forget about chores and they won't get done.

You were going to do your chore today but when you went to get the broom, it was missing. You tried to get the other boys to help you find it but they wouldn't help and said you probably lost it. That got you upset and now you are worried you will be in trouble for losing the broom and not getting your chores done. Your chore remains undone and the broom is missing.

(3)   **Find a solution.** The care worker can promote discovery and learning by inviting the child to collaborate and find a solution that will satisfy all concerns.

Example: How can we get the chores done and give you time to pull yourself together after a disappointing day at school? Let's look at the schedule and see what else we have to accomplish today.

We still have chores, we do not know where the broom is, and you are worried about being in trouble. Can we think of some ways to get chores done and make sure that you don't get into trouble?

This strategy can be used to prevent situations from escalating and can also prevent problems. Care workers have ample information about children's patterns of behavior in order to anticipate when there might be some rough patches ahead. Using this simple problem-solving method can prevent children from getting into situations where they cannot meet expectations and teaches them to solve problems.

Option: Use Consequences

When frustrated and upset, care workers may fantasize about finding the right reward or punishment that would magically change the child's behavior. Our entire society seems to be stuck on the idea that if the reward is attractive enough or the punishment is severe enough, it is possible to get people to behave as demanded. In one sense this is a true statement. If people are afraid enough or motivated enough, they will try to comply and try to do what is asked; nothing more, nothing less. And they will do it as long as they can earn the reward or avoid the punishment. They will be temporarily obedient and compliant. Their motivation will be to get the reward or avoid the punishment and the behavior (lesson) that is being reinforced, is forgotten (Kohn, 1993). The game becomes, *How can I do this and not get caught?* This will impede children's natural desire to master new skills and develop competencies. When discussing consequences, it is helpful to look at what it is care workers want to teach and what are the long-term goals for the children. Is it obedience or self-control (for example, dependency on external motivators or values and beliefs about how people should be in the world, taking responsibility for one's own actions or blind conformity?).

As stated previously, no reasonable person would punish a child for being physically hurt (for example, not completing chores because of a broken leg). Punishment is not appropriate for pain-based behavior, behavior that is a result of physical, emotional or psychological pain. In addition, punishing children who have been abused or neglected, have low self-worth and low self-efficacy only devalues them and reinforces their feelings of inadequacy and rejection. Consequences that are used in residential care must be natural or logical and offered only as a motivational tool. If the child does not realize that what he or she is doing is inappropriate, consequences might be useful. In that case, they would only need to be used once and behavior will stop, lesson learned.

When To Use Consequences

By definition, consequences are something that happens after the fact. If a child is to learn from consequences (positive or negative), the learning occurs after the event and must be learned well enough that the child (1) can remember it, (2) be motivated by it and, (3) use alternative behaviors the next time the same situation presents itself. This means that the child must already have the skills necessary to handle the situation more appropriately. The child must be able, but not willing. It also implies that the child can remember the lesson learned from the consequences and that the idea of the same consequences the next time is a strong enough motivator to change the behavior. Using consequences as a strategy is a motivational tool. As Ross Greene (2001) states, "Motivational strategies don't make the impossible possible; they make the possible more possible."

(1)   The child has demonstrated the ability to meet the expectation in the past.

(2)   The expectation is reasonable.

(3)   The child will remember the consequence and be motivated by it when faced with the same situation. (See Table 6.)

Table 6. Use Consequences

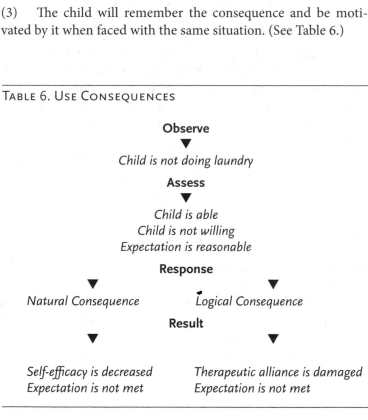

Observe
▼
Child is not doing laundry

Assess
▼
Child is able
Child is not willing
Expectation is reasonable

Response
▼   ▼
Natural Consequence   *Logical Consequence*

Result
▼   ▼

Self-efficacy is decreased   *Therapeutic alliance is damaged*
Expectation is not met   *Expectation is not met*

Response Techniques That Use Natural Consequences

Do nothing—natural consequences are just that—natural. They occur as a result of the action or inaction of the child. Children can learn from the results of their actions.

Example: Johnnie doesn't do his chore and the floor remains dirty. The children hassle him about how dirty the floor is. When the supervisor arrives, comments are made about how dirty the room looks. If Johnnie cares about how others think about him, he will sweep the floor. The next day when Johnnie sweeps the floor, it is twice as much work since it is extra dirty. It takes a long time and Johnnie misses his favorite program on TV.

Response Techniques That Use Logical Consequences

Whenever possible, logical consequences should be agreed upon by the community of children and adults who live, work, and play in the life space. Once agreed upon, they can be referred to in advance and also applied after the fact.

Example: If you refuse to wear your seat belt, you cannot ride in the van. If you break the lamp, you must replace it. If you do not put your bicycle away, you cannot ride it tomorrow.

Remind child of program consequences. Establish consequences that are a logical response to a child's behavior. These consequences could reflect what might happen eventually, but not immediately.

Example: Remind Johnnie that if he doesn't do his chores, he won't get his entire allowance on Saturday since it is based on completing chores.

Let the consequences stand. Once established and understood, allow the behavior to occur and apply the consequences after the fact.

Example: Johnnie gets a reduced allowance on Saturday.

Teachers or Jailors

A difficult but essential task for care workers is to make a decision as to whether they want to help children learn self-regulation skills and pro-social behaviors by teaching, modeling, coaching, and mentoring, or if they want to enforce rules and demand obedience and compliance. When children are not behaving as desired, what role will the care worker assume? What is the long-term goal for the child? Helping children learn self-regulation skills increases their resiliency and improves their ability to develop positively (Gardner et al., 2008; Gestsdottir & Lerner, 2008). Helping the child overcome obstacles and learn important life skills is in the child's best interest and must be the primary concern and focus of the care worker.

Summary

When a child in care fails to meet expectations, it is a care worker's responsibility to figure out why the child has failed and what the worker can do to help the child meet the expectation the next time around. When a child is not behaving as desired, the worker should first look and listen to assess the situation, then think about what the child needs in order to meet expectations (or if the expectation should be dropped for the time being), and then respond appropriately to help the child.

A worker has five general options when responding to a child's needs: the first is to acknowledge the behavior when the child is meeting expectations, encourage the child to meet the expectation by prompting, offering assistance, orienting the child to the future, or appealing to good decision-making. Another option for workers is to teach the child how to manage in the situation better by listening to and validating the child to figure out what the difficulty is, defining the problem, and finding a solution that will satisfy all involved. The worker can change or drop the expectation when the situation is overwhelming. The final option for care workers is to use consequences—an option that should only be used when a worker feels the child will learn from, remember, and be motivated by the consequence. Consequences may be natural—those that follow directly from a child's actions—or logical—those agreed upon by the care community and made in advance. When a child is not meeting expectations, the goal of the care worker is to figure out how to help the child meet the expectation. ✿

Striving for the Ordinary in Residential care

CHAPTER *16*

The Everyday and Ordinary in Residential Care

It is within the minutiae of life and not in the big events that one's personal pursuits and direction are determined.

—Henry Maier

The day-to-day interactions among children and adults, the daily events of work and play, time spent alone day dreaming or reflecting, the accomplishment of routine tasks, are the central components of one's life experience in residential care or at home (Anglin, 2002; Maier, 1987; Ward, 2004). All children need normal developmental experiences that allow them to feel included, similar to others, and valued for who they are and what they contribute to the *family*. Through these ordinary life experiences, children develop a sense of belonging, trust, competence, and autonomy. A common goal for all children in care is developing a "sense of normality" (Anglin, 2002). A sense of normality does not mean being *normal* or complying with a set of social or developmental norms. This is not only unrealistic for children in residential care, but also inappropriate. Developing a sense of normality means providing children with opportunities to experience and develop the capacity to understand and appreciate aspects of normal family and community life.

Residential care facilities cannot pretend to be a *normal* family nor would it be helpful if they did. Children are placed in residential care because they cannot handle the pressures and intimacy of a familial situation or the demands of the community setting. Good residential care can offer transitional and approximating experiences that will prepare children for a return to the family and community (Anglin, 2002). The concept of "normalization" has been a central theme in residential care for several decades (Maier, 1987; Wolfensberger, 1972). Providing typical and healthy experiences as close as possible to each child's community norms helps provide a bridge for the child to return to his or her community. Although this concept is simple, it can be difficult to implement and may threaten the status quo of an organization. Creating experiences that take into account the child's world-view and zone of proximal development demands a reasoned and planned approach.

Anglin (2002) identified a variety of ways that residential group care could apply the concept of normality in everyday life.

Residential home routines. Normalization might mean establishing a normal rhythm for the week, the year, the day. There is a difference between school days and weekends, school year and summer vacation. Regular chores, normal bedtimes based on the child's age, weekday or weekend, meals eaten family style, clearing the table, can all approximate family life.

Residential home appearance. Pictures on the wall, lamps on the tables, posters and family portraits in the bedrooms are ways to soften the institutional look and provide a more *home-like* feel and appearance. Rules and restrictions posted on the walls create an institutional, restrictive atmosphere. Furniture arranged in small groupings invite personal discussion and interaction.

Child behavior. All staff members should understand and be familiar with what is developmentally "normal" behavior for the children in their care. Children should be encouraged and have opportunities to behave like their contemporaries in the community. This may range from running around in circles with a sheet draped across their shoulders pretending to be superheroes, to spending long periods of time in front of a mirror combing their hair. Borrowing another girl's makeup, losing a shoe, being late for a meal, are normal occurrences and can be used to help children grow and develop along normal developmental pathways. Children need assistance to learn how to be a *normal* teenager or *normal* 9-year-old. Their appearance should be similar to their peers in the community.

Family-like functioning. Some aspects of group care can simulate the interactions and experiences of *family life*. Discussing each person's day at the dinner table, developing reciprocal relationships, helping children learn to care for others and give to the family are examples of how families function. Using language that reflects family or *normal* conversations instead of institutional terms or jargon when having conversations provides a sense of normalcy. Having real responsibility to others, contributing to the group, participating in decisionmaking within one's abilities are additional ways to provide for *family-like* experiences without pretending to be a family.

Socially acceptable behavior. If children are to develop the skills and resources they need to live in the community (social competence) and become a well-functioning adult, they need opportunities to try out new skills and experience *normal* interactions and daily tasks. Eating in a restaurant, shopping for clothes, and playing ball at the community center are everyday experiences for children at home and in the community. Every child's life ought to be as close as possible to the life experiences of his or her peers in the community.

Providing these normalizing experiences within the child's zone of proximal development and in the context of group care is a challenge for the organization and care worker. Many of these daily routines and functions are *institutionalized* for convenience and cost savings (for example, on grounds store, clothing bought in bulk and distributed, cafeteria style dining). Individualizing experiences in a group is always a difficult but necessary task. Some children in the group will be able to manage some of the normalizing routines better than others. Some children will need individualized support in coping with the simplest of daily tasks. Providing ordinary and everyday experiences for children in group care requires careful planning and special support based on individual children's needs and development. ✿

CHAPTER *17*

The Ecology of Human Development

If you bungle raising your children, I don't think whatever else you do well matters very much.

—*Jacqueline Kennedy Onassis*

Children do not stand still. Each day a child grows physically, cognitively, emotionally, and behaviorally. Fortunately, development is biased toward competence. Children are inclined to actively engage in their environment, eager to learn new skills, as long as they experience pleasurable outcomes. Children continue to develop and learn motivated by the pleasure of mastering new skills (Benard, 2004; Masten & Coatsworth, 1998; Jones, 2001). The developmental process, while driven from within, is influenced and guided from without. What the child becomes will be determined in part by external influences. Children are active, growing, and developing in their environment.

Development is influenced by the interactions among the child, the people, and the environment (Bronfenbrenner, 1979). Children's developmental experiences in a dangerous inner city are different than in a rural setting. Poverty can greatly interfere with a child's positive development if the child's parents are financially and emotionally stressed. This leaves little energy or time for parent-child interactions that enhance the child's development.

Based on the culture and the community, people may have different values and expectations for the child's development of competence. What helps a child survive in one setting might put them at risk in another. When assessing a child's level of competence, it is important to consider the environment in which the child has lived.

Developmental Tasks

What common criteria are used to decide how well a child is growing and developing? Generally, expectations for growth and development are set by criteria known as developmental tasks. Over the years, much research (Erikson, Piaget, Kohlberg, Gilligan, Greenspan, Freud, Goleman) has been conducted to identify specific developmental tasks necessary for children to achieve in different areas in order to develop into competent adults. These areas include cognitive, social, emotional, physical, sexual, and moral development. Table 7. Developmental Tasks, outlines some examples of developmental tasks based on the child's age and the developmental domain (category).

Infancy and Childhood

For infants and young children, key developmental tasks occur in the context of the close relationships with adults in the parenting role. That relationship and the security it provides profoundly influence the child's ability to achieve developmental milestones. Disruptions in these relationships can have a dramatic effect on the child's growth and development. The following is a very brief synopsis of general expectations of infants and children at different stages.

Infant (0-2 years). During infancy the child is growing rapidly, learning to crawl, walk, and going through many biological changes. Emotionally, attachment with the primary caregiver(s) is the dominant social and emotional task for the infant. This sets the stage for developing trusting relationships later in life. Regarding moral development, in the eyes of the child, whatever the child wants is right or good, what the child does not want is wrong or bad.

Toddler (2-4 years). Toddlers are preoccupied with their own bodies and bodily functions. Their motor control improves as they learn to run and climb. They become much more independent as they are able to do more and demand to do more and more on their own such as dress themselves, pour their own milk, and so on. Their social world expands as the extended family and neighborhood becomes more important. They begin to learn how to play with others, usually starting out with parallel play activities. Toddlers have very short attention spans; they begin to learn about cause-and-effect, and understand basic right and wrong. Children at this age believe that if the adult says it is right, it is right; if the adult says it is wrong, it is wrong.

Early Childhood (4-6 years)

As children continue to grow, they become more and more aware of their bodies and differences between the sexes. Children 4-6 years old are very active physically. They are normally very curious about everything and they express curiosity about sexual matters through play. Their social world expands greatly as they go to school, play with others, and learn to share. Their communication skills improve as language expands. At this age, children are very interested in pleasing adults and want to do right and avoid wrong.

TABLE 7. DEVELOPMENTAL TASKS

Developmental Stage & Task	Physical/Sexual Development
Infant (0-2 years) Trust	Oral needs, rapid growth and biological change, crawling, walking
Toddler (2-4 years) Autonomy *(Self-sufficiency)*	Motor control, runs, controls bowels and bladder, feeds self, interested in own body
Early Childhood (4-6 years) Initiative *(Act and make decisions on their own)*	Very active, rapid muscle growth, aware of sex differences, explores own body
Middle Childhood (6-10 years) Industry *(Individual accomplishment)*	Physical growth slows, increased physical power and skills, interested in sex play and experimentation
Early Adolescence (10-14 years) Identity	Puberty, sexual urges, rapid growth and body changes, secondary sex characteristics, acne
Adolescence (15-19 years) Identity	Physical maturation completed, increased probability of acting on sexual desires

Social/Emotional Development	Intellectual/Moral Development
Primary caregiver figure dominates, trust, bonding	Routines, rewards, repetition, consistency, what child wants is right
Primary caregiver, family, neighborhood, temper tantrums, begins group play	Fast cognitive growth, short attention span, physical realities, cause-and-effect, begins to know right and wrong
Plays with others, learns to share, language is essential for social interaction, wants to please adults	Extremely curious, wants to do right and avoid wrong, may blame others for wrong doing
Identifies with adults outside of family, school friends, compares self to others, cooperative group play, associates with same sex	Eager for learning, develops hobbies, experiences guilt and shame, logical thinking, concepts, conscience develops, fairness is important
Critical of adults, has best friend, privacy, peers, likes competitive games and teams, clubs, moody, worries, introspective	Strong sense of justice and moral code, knows right and wrong
Dates, may have romantic relationship, many friends, mood swings	Confused and disappointed in value/behavior discrepancies, concerned with future, creative, thinks abstractly

Middle Childhood (6-10 years)

During middle childhood, children's physical growth slows down and they begin to develop increased physical power and skills. Group play skills continue to develop as children learn to cooperate with peers, problem-solve, and, through play, begin to develop friendships. Although group interaction is extremely important at this age, friendships are unstable and group loyalty is fleeting until later in this stage when they become much more peer-oriented and move more toward impressing their friends than adults. There is some competition at this age as children learn to measure their own worth by comparing themselves to others of the same age. Children need to develop a sense of accomplishment centered on the ability to learn and apply skills, deal with peers, compete, and exhibit self-control. They are eager to learn, they begin to think logically, and they develop a sense of fairness that becomes a central concern.

Adolescence

Biological processes and social influences drive many aspects of adolescence. No stage of development requires as much adjustment as does adolescence since nothing about young people stays the same during this period. Adolescents' bodies are rapidly changing, their emotions and feelings change dramatically, their relationships with family and peers all take on new meaning and change. The adolescent's ideas about the entire world change. The following is a very brief summary of general expectations of adolescents at different ages.

Early adolescence (10-14 years). Puberty comes at this stage of development, bringing with it a dramatic change in the child's body. Usually there is a growth spurt, sexual organs begin to mature and function, and there are many secondary sex changes. Bones grow faster than muscle and often adolescents become quite clumsy. The drastic changes in body hormones that accompany sexual development may cause exciting, frightening, and confusing sexual and aggressive impulses. This has a profound effect on the adolescent's emotional stability, often resulting in mood swings. Emotions are exaggerated and extreme.

Ten to 12-year-olds enter intense same-sex friendships. Fear or uneasy feelings about sexuality at this time often cause children to deny any affinity for the opposite sex at all. They are likely to experiment with *dirty language* and body comparisons. As the adolescent grows older, relationships with members of the opposite sex take on more importance.

Young adolescents usually develop a strong sense of justice and know right from wrong. They have developed a moral code and react strongly when it has been violated. Since changes in thinking ability occur gradually, it is normal for adolescents to be able to think abstractly and reflectively in one area and to be tied to concrete thought in another. For example, an adolescent may be capable of mature thought about justice, religion, or higher mathematics, but unable to comprehend the risks involved in sexual intercourse without protection. Important skills or information need to be conveyed in a variety of ways.

The adolescent's social group is mostly composed of peers. This group replaces the family as a source for setting expectations for behavior and of experiencing a sense of belonging. Adolescents need to develop satisfying and healthy relationships with friends of both sexes. They need to develop the ability to be independent of adults. Adolescents may feel socially awkward and strive to obtain a certain grace and poise in their social behaviors. While the peer group can be a source of negative influence in some situations for some adolescents, involvement with friends is necessary if youth are to become socially competent adults.

Later adolescence (15-19 years). During this period, physical maturation is completed and there is an increased probability that the older adolescent will act on sexual desires, as he or she explores different relationships in preparation for a life mate. They may have many romantic relationships and experience many mood swings.

Adolescents feel that they are supremely important and unique and that no one knows how they feel and/or understands them. There is also a feeling of loneliness. Adolescents begin to break out of these forms of selfishness as they grow and mature. In building close mutual relationships with other adolescents and sharing innermost concerns and dreams, they begin to realize that other people experience life somewhat as they do.

Adolescents feel a sense of immortality. Bad things happen to other people, not to them or to those close to them. This may result in dangerous risk-taking behavior by adolescents who believe they are immune to the consequences of their actions and invulnerable to harm. As they gain life experiences and observe the harm that befalls others because of dangerous behavior, they begin to realize that they are not immune to the consequences of their actions.

Older adolescents become concerned with the future and have the ability to think abstractly. They are easily disappointed in discrepancies between values and behaviors and become confused when these events occur. Adolescents experience an increased ability to think creatively and to reason. During this time of development, the ability to think about abstract ideas such as truth, reality, and acceptance leads them to explore facts and theories, and objectively interpret situations and reality. Behavior becomes based more upon duty and conscience than pleasure and ego satisfaction. Adolescents begin to be guided by moral responsibility and ideals rather than being dependent upon positive reinforcement.

Special Tasks of Adolescents

There are four special developmental tasks that adolescents must accomplish in order to become healthy, functioning adults (Feldman & Elliott, 1990; Prothrow-Stith & Weissman, 1993):

(1)   Separating from family. Adolescents begin to see themselves as persons separate from their family. This can be an intense emotional struggle with countless arguments about freedom, responsibility, and control. The peer group becomes the reference group. This can be an advantage or present problems based on the peer group and the adolescent's ability to separate when necessary.

(2)   Forming a healthy sexual identity. Adolescents must learn to manage their romantic and sexual feelings. They must learn to relate to and value a romantic partner. A number of influences hinder adolescents' abilities to develop satisfying, nonviolent, permanent relationships. These include the media, the rate of teenage pregnancies, sexually transmitted infections, and single parent families.

(3)   Preparing for the future. Having a future gives an adolescent a reason for trying to achieve goals and for valuing his or her life and those of others. School and extra-curricular activities help the adolescent prepare for the future. They give young people an opportunity to devote themselves to something other than themselves. Adolescents also need adult mentors—role models—who can inspire them.

(4)   Developing a moral value system. Moral reasoning develops jointly with cognitive abilities, although it involves thinking and feeling. Adolescents must move beyond Kohlberg's Stage 1 and 2 levels of moral reasoning. Stage 1 children are motivated by fear of punishment or retaliation. Stage 2 is the self-interest stage (usually preadolescence) in which the child is motivated by what is in it for himself or herself. Stage 3 is the safe zone where adolescents can see the moral and legal context and implications in situations. They can see the intricacies in the world and understand how rules/laws benefit the community as well as the individual.

Competent care workers engage children in activities that are within the child's developmental ability and readiness to grow. They help children develop and maintain relationships, skills, and a sense of identity that will help the child grow into a competent and productive adult. ✿

CHAPTER 18

Growing Up in Care

"Dost thou love life?" Ben Franklin once asked.
"Then do not squander time, for that is the stuff life is made of."

When children are placed in group care, they do not stop developing, they do not stand still. When they arrive in care, the environment they have lived in has had a huge impact on their development. Equally true is that the residential environment they are now in can have a tremendous impact on their future development. The organization must garner its resources to facilitate each child's growth and development.

Early Developmental Life Experiences

Early childhood experiences set the foundation for the child's ability to develop skills in later life. Many children in care have experienced conditions such as poverty, racism, abuse, neglect, family violence, and substance abuse that inhibit healthy development. Part of developing an identity comes from a socialization process that involves the community, the society, and the cultural reference group. Being a member of a minority group, such as youth of color, poor youth, youth with disabilities, and gay and lesbian youth, presents enormous challenges for positive identity formation in a society that devalues them. Children of color are very often placed in care without minority staff members present. All of these children face special problems with identity formation and need supportive environments to explore matters of ethnic/racial and gender identity issues.

Experiences such as poverty, abuse, neglect, and substance abuse may also affect brain development. The development of the brain is profoundly influenced by experience and traumatic events, which has many implications for intervention strategies (Cicchetti & Tucker, 1994; Nelson, 2002). As children develop and learn new behaviors, they are dependent on the ability of their brain to adapt. Children need opportunities to try out new skills and problem-solve new situations to help develop the decision-making/planning function of the brain. Strategies that help this process are teaching new skills in deficit areas, opportunities for the child to practice these new skills successfully, and adapting the environment so the child can succeed.

Resiliency and Protective Factors

As discussed previously, all children have the same basic requirements for growth and development, but progress varies from child to child, in part, based on life experiences. Children in care need support and opportunities that engage their innate capacity to grow and develop. Resiliency research has identified personal strengths or competencies that are associated with healthy development and life success that appear to be universal (Benard, 2004; Brendtro et al., 1998; Werner, 1990). These strengths include: social competency, including relationship and attachment skills, problem-solving skills, autonomy and self-efficacy, and sense of purpose or meaning. These strengths are developed through normal developmental processes and positive and supportive interactions in the environment. Resiliency does not come from special gifts or qualities, but from everyday, normal opportunities for growth and development. All human beings have the innate capacity to develop relationships, problem-solve, develop a positive identity and autonomy, and have hope for the future and meaning to their lives. With protective factors in their environment and opportunities for normal developmental experiences, children, even in the face of adversity, can achieve success in their lives.

In a nurturing environment, the innate developmental capacity of children can be engaged. A nurturing environment is one that meets the children's needs for belonging, safety, autonomy and competence, all contributing to a sense of hope for the future. Specific environmental factors that create nurturing environments are caring relationships, high expectation messages, and opportunities for participation and contribution (Benard, 2004).

Caring relationships. All of the qualities previously discussed that help form attachments and build therapeutic relationships are part of caring relationships. Compassionate care workers are interested in and listen to children. Supportive and caring relationships are the key to healthy development and provide an environment where children can thrive.

High expectation messages. Not only do care workers need to give children clear expectations to create a structure and sense of safety, but they need to communicate their belief that the children can succeed and achieve their hopes and dreams. Being treated and seen as a competent and capable person helps build the child's self-efficacy and has a self-fulfilling function.

Opportunities for participation and contribution. Opportunities for cooperative activities, decisionmaking, creative endeavors, problem-solving, discussion, reflection, contribution, and helping others provide children with a medium for developing skills, a positive identity, and a positive sense of the future. Children learn by doing and being involved in successful learning opportunities.

Summary

All children need normal developmental experiences. Through these ordinary life experiences, children develop a sense of belonging, trust, competency, and autonomy. A common goal for all children in care is developing a *sense of normality*. Providing typical and healthy experiences helps provide a bridge for children to return to their communities.

At every age, children have developmental tasks that are necessary for them to accomplish in order to develop into competent adults. Cognitive, emotional, physical, sexual, and moral gains must be made in order to achieve this goal. Any hindrance in the environment that gets in the way of normal development may affect children for years to come, though some gains may be made up at later stages. One of the goals of good residential care is to provide children with the optimal social, physical, and emotional environment in which to reach developmental tasks and grow into healthy adults.

All children in care bring with them a past history that may include experiences of poverty, discrimination, abuse, neglect, and substance abuse. One of the primary goals of residential care is to help children recover what they may have lost through these conditions and experiences by providing the support and opportunities that engage their innate capacity to grow and develop.

In a nurturing environment, the innate developmental capacity of children can be engaged. Specific environmental factors that create nurturing environments are caring relationships, high expectation messages, and opportunities for participation and contribution. ✿

THE RHYTHM OF CARING

CHAPTER 19
The Rhythm of Caring

In the absence of clearly defined goals, we become strangely loyal to performing daily trivia until ultimately we become enslaved by it.

—*Robert Heinlein*

When people dance, play ping-pong, toss a ball, they are momentarily connected and have a sense of unity. These are rhythmic interactions that forge people together and provide the glue for human connections (Krueger, 1994; Maier, 1992). Rhythmic activities provide the experience of repetition and continuity with the promise of predictability, important elements in providing a safe environment for developing trusting relationships. Care workers can use this rhythmicity by engaging in rhythmic interactions and rituals to help build relationships and help children experience a sense of unity and stability.

Establishing Structure, Routines, and Expectations

Creating a therapeutic milieu involves finding a healthy balance between providing adequate structure to help children feel safe and secure and having enough flexibility to meet the constantly changing needs of children and young people. The day's events, from waking to bedtime, make up a young person's life experiences during placement. Because all young people are greatly influenced by their life experiences, the daily activities in the agency milieu can stimulate learning and skill development by carefully considering the needs of the young people. The day's events can be used to increase coping abilities, strengthen defenses, prevent frustration, and increase self-control, as well as develop important daily living skills and routines that foster the development of healthy personal habits. Daily routines and activities can also teach children to negotiate every day tasks with increasing competence and independence.

Unfortunately, strict rigid routines that serve the needs of the organization instead of the children living there, can depersonalize care and create problems between the staff and young people (Bettleheim, 1950; Mohr et al., 2009; Redl and Wineman, 1952; Trieschman et al., 1969; Weiner, 1991). It is critical that care workers remember that the goals of daily routines and activities are to help children feel safe and secure, develop relationships with staff, achieve developmental milestones, and build competencies.

Children and young people in general, and children in care even more so, need to be engaged in enjoyable, rewarding, and meaningful activities and routines that meet their needs. Basic routines that are predictable will provide order and stability in children's lives. It is important for children to know when they will eat, go to bed, and go to school. These transition times are especially difficult for children who often feel a loss of control when they move from one activity to another. Structuring these times of the day can help them develop trust with the adults and comfort with the environment. Routines provide a framework for the predictable satisfaction of basic needs. Children can count on the care workers and depend on specific things to happen at set times.

Routines

Well-designed routines have the following elements (Alwon, Budlong, Holden, Holden, Kuhn, & Mooney et al., 1988):

A predictable, consistent structure and expectations for behavior. Routines clearly outline the minimal expectations for children in care. They also set the boundaries for children so that they can experiment and take risks within those boundaries. The routines are there regardless of which care worker is on duty. This helps provide consistent expectations from all staff members and depersonalizes limit setting. Getting through the routines is not a test of the personal relationship of staff and children. It is not a care worker *making* children do something. It is a basic expectation.

Enough flexibility to accommodate individual needs of children. Some children may take longer to get ready for school than others. The routine for this child might include being awakened a few minutes before the other children. A routine should help the child meet daily expectations by setting up a schedule that facilitates the child's ability to achieve daily expectations. Routines should help build competence, not demand compliance or cause overwhelming frustration and stress. Designing routines within each child's zone of proximal development helps children build competence and avoids conflict and crises.

Good habits that meet the needs of the children. Routines should teach good habits that children can use the rest of their lives. Routines must be established to meet the needs of the children, not to make things convenient for the staff or organization. If routines are designed appropriately, they help care workers teach young people how to make use of limited time and set reasonable expectations for necessary daily tasks (such as waking up, showering, eating breakfast, and getting to school on time).

A balance between individual and group needs. This is not an easy task. It means that routines are never set in stone. They should be continually assessed for their appropriateness and usefulness to the individuals and the group. If they are not helping teach competency and helping children get through the day, then modifications or elimination of the routine may be in order. The children may need more structure or less structure. Being flexible and meeting children's changing needs takes good observation, assessment, and teamwork skills.

Segments that partition the child's day into manageable, identifiable parts. Children with limited coping skills will manage better if the day is broken up into smaller time periods than if they face the day in its entirety. This alone can prevent major melt-downs. Step-by-step routines provide clear instructions and expectations and can lower anxiety around the who, when, and where of children's problems.

Everyone needs routines and structure to their days, some more than others. There are also certain times of the day that will need to be managed with sensitivity and care. Well-designed routines, according to Maslow (1969), play a central role in helping meet basic physiological and safety needs, as well as provide the foundation for belonging. Routines and structure should be used as a progression of guidelines, boundaries, and expectations that change as the children grow and change.

For routines to help build competencies, the care worker needs to help the child see the connection between everyday activities (such as cleaning the bedroom), and becoming a competent person. If there are no connections between the routine and building important competencies for life, there is a question as to the necessity of the routine. If the child is afraid to go to school, is compulsive about bathing, or always feels sick, the care worker and the team need to find ways to help work through these concerns through routines and daily living activities.

Morning Routine

There seem to be two kinds of children in the world—those who get up before they should in the morning, and those who get up after they should. Waking up and the morning routine set the tone for the rest of the day and need to be carefully planned and executed for the day to get off to a smooth start. When children and young people have been asleep, some happily dreaming and some with nightmares, they must transition from nice warm, safe beds to a world of interaction, stress, and demands. Anyone who has been away from home in an institutional setting (for example, in hospitals, in military service, or at camp) knows what it is like to wake up in a strange place full of strangers. Many children wake up and are reminded that yesterday was a day full of problems or disappointments. The bad feelings can flood back and make it difficult to face a new day. This is a major transition for children and care workers, who therefore should begin the morning routine as quietly and gently as possible.

Suggestions that make the morning routine, as well as all routines, run smoothly include:

Individualize the routine. Wake children individually, according to their preferences, in a sensitive and caring fashion (Mayer, 1978). A staff member who calmly walks into a youth's room and uses a calm, re-assuring tone of voice for the wake-up call, is setting the tone for the morning.

Allow adequate time. The morning routine should allow adequate time for tasks to be successfully completed before the young person heads off to school. Eating breakfast, bathing, making the bed, and getting to school are reasonable and necessary tasks to complete. Some children may need more time than others to get through the morning routine. It is important that the time allowed for the morning routine does not rush children or result in long waiting periods. Either one can be a trigger for frustration and acting out behaviors. Children should head off to school ready to face the day, not frustrated and angry or overly stressed.

Be aware of and responsive to the child's developmental needs. Depending on the age and developmental level of the child, privacy is an important concern. Respect goes a long way in demonstrating sensitivity, understanding, and acceptance. Demonstrating proper etiquette by knocking on the door before entering a bedroom is good modeling. Allowing privacy during showers and personal hygiene tasks is important, especially for children who may have special concerns such as body image issues or bedwetting.

Ensuring privacy and safety presents challenges for the care staff, especially during morning and evening routines. Care workers need to closely monitor the children while not invading their privacy. Maintaining good relationships and coordinating the routines with co-workers is essential to make this a successful time of the day.

Meal Times

Food is more than a necessary part of keeping a human being alive; it is laden with emotional, psychological, cultural, and social values (Mayer, 1958). Teaching children to eat nutritional food that will keep them healthy is an important part of meal times. A variety of values must be considered when planning, preparing, serving, and eating food in residential care.

Nutritional value. All programs have standards in place for ensuring the children in care receive proper, balanced meals throughout the day. This is important for healthy development. For many young people, eating a healthy and nutritional meal is a new experience and, like any new experience, it can be stressful.

Care workers need to be sensitive to the anxiety the children may experience when faced with *foreign food*.

Psychological value. Children who have experienced neglect and abuse may associate some of these experiences around mealtimes. Children who have not had enough to eat may hoard food. Children may have found comfort in food and over eat which may result in weight problems. Helping children eat healthy and nutritional meals, or confronting children who steal or hoard food, may result in power struggles between the care workers and children. To avoid these struggles and be helpful, staff must explore beyond the behavior and get to the feelings and needs of the children.

Social value. Bringing the staff and children together for mealtime offers a great opportunity for learning through modeling. For many children, these are new experiences that were never evidenced in their own homes. Practicing appropriate table manners and how to engage in dinner conversation are ways to help children master important social skills and provide a *normal* environment.

Food should never be used as a form of punishment or reinforcement. Food is a basic need, not a privilege. Eating good food should be a pleasurable experience. Food that tastes good should also be nutritional.

Bedtime Routines

The bedtime routine signals the conclusion of the day's program activities and the preparation for the end of the day. Successful bedtime routines are predictable and designed to reduce stimulation (Trieschman et al., 1969). The lights begin to lower, the noise level is reduced, children may have a snack, take a shower, and engage in quiet activities that lead to getting into bed and lights out.

This is a vulnerable time of day and if one child is experiencing stress, it can lead to other children becoming stressed and the entire routine can be disrupted. It is important to think ahead and plan carefully so that children do not begin activities that they cannot finish (such as a television program, or involvement in an activity that can increase stress such as a competitive game).

Bedtime may also cause emotional/psychological distress for some children. It is a time when they are alone with their thoughts and can be reminded of unpleasant experiences from their past. Children who have been sexually abused may have difficulty at this time of the day. The care worker needs to remain calm and supportive when helping children cope with their fears at night, avoid getting into heavy counseling sessions or conversations, and help children get to sleep.

Transition Times

Transitions include those in-between times that take place when moving from one activity to the next and that represent beginnings and endings. Children with certain developmental disabilities and children who have experienced many disruptions in their lives will have difficulties with transitions. It is important to plan carefully for the many transitions throughout the day.

Abruptly ending an activity or asking children to line up to move from one activity to another is a common source of frustration and often contributes to the breakdown of the group. Care workers can help the group move from one activity to another by using their relationship and creativity. Engaging children in energizing activities, such as tossing a ball or playing follow the leader, or having a discussion about the activity that is ending and what the expectations are for the next activity, are all methods used to successfully transition children from one activity to the next.

Rituals and Traditions

Rituals help young people to feel they belong in a world where they may otherwise feel alienated. "To be alienated is to lack a sense of belonging, to feel cut off from family, friends, school, and work—the four worlds of childhood" (Bronfenbrenner, 1979, p. 430). Ceremony and ritual give order, stability, and confidence to youth in care (Hobbs, 1975). It is important to create traditions and rituals, such as how the group celebrates holidays, birthdays, or individual and group successes and achievements. Rituals and traditions can be established in a unit or for the entire organization. It is a way to include children in the group and help them attach to each other by providing for common experiences. Some ceremonies and rituals can also provide peak experience opportunities that are important for developing relationships and groups. ✿

CHAPTER 20

More Than Bricks and Mortar: The Creative Use of Space

...a house that smiles, props which invite, and space which allows.

—Fritz Redl

The environment that surrounds the young people in the care setting can have a profound influence on their behavior. A young person coming into residential care is entering a different culture. It is critical to be sensitive to each young person's background and help the young person integrate into the new *culture* while maintaining ties to home. The diversity of the cultural and ethnic backgrounds of the children should be easily observed throughout the living space.

The way children and young people arrange their belongings in their individual space will speak volumes about their values, priorities, and feelings. Simply walking into the young person's room is a valuable assessment tool. How children maintain their space and display their belongings can assist a care worker in understanding how the child is feeling, what the child values, and some of the hopes the child has. Is the child encouraged to personalize his or her space with pictures from home or a favorite poster? Allowing the children to personalize their space will help them feel like they belong and have a place that is their own where they feel safe. As discussed previously, these are extremely important needs for all children and even more so for children in residential care.

Physical Setting

The physical environment should be comfortable, have appropriate furnishings for children and young people and adequate space for play and activities. The physical environment should be arranged to invite the types of interactions and behaviors that are desired. One of the main jobs children have in order to grow and develop is to play. Is there room to play? Are there *props* that encourage play? Is there time for play? The way the agency and the care workers maintain the environment tells a story about the care given to the young people. Is it calming and nurturing?

Two common elements in the environment that can have a stimulating or calming effect on young people are lighting and noise. Bright, harsh, ceiling lighting is more stimulating than soft table lamps. Trying to study in a room with inadequate lighting adds frustration to an already difficult task. Likewise, the noise level can contribute to the overall tranquility or excitement of the group. Holding a group discussion with the television on or music blaring makes a statement of the importance of the meeting.

Space Influences Daily Interactions

Physical arrangements can either enhance or inhibit daily activities. What does the spatial arrangement encourage? Discourage? Are there places for groups to gather? Can children find a place to be alone and take a break from interactions? Are staff offices away from where the children gather? Is there pushing and shoving when children enter the dining area? Could this be caused by inadequate space at the entry way or too much furniture in the area? Rarely do care workers have input into the design of a building, but they may have the ability to adapt what is there and change the use of space. Does the spatial arrangement advance the objectives of the program? Change the space and change the interactions and flow of children's activities.

Private Versus Public Space

Children need private space that they can claim as their own territory. A person's position and value to an organization is very often defined by the space they have as their own. Compare the size of an executive's office with other offices. Private space is not only needed to verify oneself and value, but to be used as a place to reflect and re-energize. All human beings occasionally wish to be alone and have space they can call their own. This is especially important when people live and work in close proximity to each other (Bettelheim, 1974; Maier, 1987). Children need private places to put their personal belongings and decorate as their place. A bed and a room have significance for everyone, but is especially important for children in care. It is a place that connotes permanence and somewhere to return at the end of the day. Arbitrary or frequent room and bed changes disregard a child's place in the group setting and communicate disregard and impermanence.

Public space should also be clearly defined. Is it the children's public space? Do all children have access to the space? What about others? Is the children's living area open to anyone who wants to walk through? Does a visitor, executive director, or maintenance worker knock before entering the unit? Does the group living area belong to the children and workers involved in their daily lives or does it belong to the community, board members, or visitors?

Personal territory defines who we are and our value and position in an organization. A sense of permanence is directly related to whether or not a person has a guaranteed private space (Maier, 1987). Public space is the arena for people to interact and engage with each other. Spatial arrangements control actions and either facilitate or hinder the goals of the program.

The environment can often be organized to minimize problems and promote order. For example, during times such as dinner or homework time, staff may purposefully sit so they can provide extra supervision and support when needed. Is there space for children and young people to get away and spend time on their own away from the group? Is there a place where they can keep their possessions safe? Based on the developmental needs of the children, can the physical environment be altered? Managing and purposefully arranging the physical environment can promote the type of interactions and activities that are desired for children to grow and develop.

Summary

Rhythmic activities, such as tossing a ball or dancing, provide the experience of repetition and continuity with the promise of predictability—important elements in providing a safe environment for developing trusting relationships. Even simple daily activities, such as waking and mealtimes, can have significant impacts on the quality of life for children in care. Having structures, routines, and expectations for various daily activities will assist in smooth transitions and can help provide the safety and structure that many children in care may have been missing in their home lives.

The way the physical environment is arranged not only affects children's behavior, but can also be used as a diagnostic tool when a worker observes the way a child has arranged his or her personal space. The residential environment should be set up to invite positive behaviors and interactions, while minimizing frustration and anxiety. It is important for children to have their personal space and be able to arrange it as they would like, within certain limits. By promoting a safe and functional space, an agency can set itself up for successful interactions in the care environment. ✿

BUILDING A CARING COMMUNITY

CHAPTER 21
Living and Learning in Groups

He drew a circle that shut me out –
Heretic, rebel, a thing to flout.
But love and I had the wit to win:
We drew a circle that took him in.

—*Edwin Markham*

Children and adolescents want to be special and they want to be just like their peers. All children want to be normal. Major tasks of care workers and everyone who works with children in residential care are to meet each child's special needs, help them feel included, and assist them in developing a sense of normality (Anglin, 2002; Maier, 1982; Ward, 2004; Wolfensberger, 1972). Group care provides the setting where this can happen by enhancing children's interactions with their peers and structuring activities that match their abilities. By providing an *ordinary environment* with normal routines, schedules, activities, school, sports, a comfortable physical environment, interactions with the community, and the measured support each child needs to manage these events, children can develop a sense of normality.

What could be more normal than being in a group? Groups are everywhere. There are family groups, school groups, social groups, and task-oriented groups. There are groups of children on playgrounds, on sports teams, in shopping centers, in the neighborhoods, and in gangs. Human beings are social beings and naturally congregate in groups. It is through these various groups that people meet a variety of needs, including the need to belong, to build competencies, and to develop a sense of self-worth. For adolescents, being part of a peer group is essential to their development. Being able to be a contributing member of a group and community is essential for a healthy adult life.

In residential care, the group setting is the context for providing care. This group setting offers a myriad of life experiences through a variety of peer groupings and contacts, encounters with a multitude of adults, and participation in diverse and rich program activities. All of these facets of group care contribute to the growth and development of the children and youth who live there. Children are strongly influenced by their relationships within their peer group and between the peer group and the group of staff (Emond, 2003; Ward, 2004). The formal and informal groups that form and reform throughout the day, all have the potential of influencing children in growth-enhancing ways. The experience of not only belonging to a group but also of helping others in a group can itself be positive and rewarding for children and youth (Bettleheim, 1950, 1974; Emond, 2003; Redl & Wineman, 1952; Vorrath & Brendtro, 1985; Ward, 2004). All of this does not happen by chance. The care worker must carefully structure, monitor, shape and guide the group process and interaction throughout the day.

Group work is to a great extent the ability to meet individual needs within a group setting. Care workers influence the overall group dynamics and emotional climate of the group and help children learn from being part of a group, using the group to develop problem-solving skills, gaining insight into how their behavior affects others, and learning interpersonal skills. By being aware of the dynamics of the group and the overall ecology of the setting (how the children are interacting in the environment), care workers can provide a structure that will keep the children active and developing within the milieu.

Group Composition

Positive group experiences do not happen by accident (Krueger, 1983; Malekoff, 1997). Care workers are responsible for managing daily routines and activities so that children will have ordinary, positive experiences that result in skill acquisition and a feeling of belonging, and a reasonable goal and purpose for group care. Sometimes care workers are expected to accomplish this goal regardless of the composition of the group. Group care is most effective when children are placed in specific groups with thought to how they will contribute to and benefit from that particular group. Mixing groups of children without careful consideration of how they interact and impact other group members can have devastating results (Arnold & Hughes, 1999; Farmer & Pollock, 1999).

Composition relates closely to need and purpose. It is expected that groups of young people in residential care will go through phases of instability and unrest. However, when composition factors continuously lead to high-risk situations and instability, then the composition of the group may need to be managed. Agencies that adopt *no reject* policies and accept children regardless of their *fit* into the group, may inadvertently set children up to be rejected by the group. The experience for the child is one of rejection, further aggravating the child's problems. These situations usually end up doing more harm than good to that child and the other children in the group.

Developing a Sense of Belonging

Can children succeed in group care if they feel they do not belong? If children do not feel accepted, they seek their own sense of *belongingness* often resulting in anti-social behavior and even gang behavior. As a result of failing to be accepted in mainstream society, many children come into care having been scapegoats, bullies, isolates, and gang members. This pattern can continue into the residential setting if care is not taken to provide positive group experiences and opportunities for children and young people to learn interpersonal skills that allow them to succeed within groups and communities. Care workers will need to skillfully manage the group to avoid removing children from group activities and discussions. If a child is continually removed or ejected from group interactions and activities, the sense of belonging is disrupted and the child continues to experience rejection and failure. Carefully managing the group, having the right mix of children, and teaching the children the skills they need to succeed within the group context will help children belong and flourish in care.

Dynamics of Group Living

One child fails a test at school. Upon returning to the group care unit, the child tosses his books across the room, knocking over a table that contained a jigsaw puzzle two children had been working on for two days. A care worker, involved in assisting another child with a science project, goes over to the upset child to find out what is bothering him. In the course of two minutes, one child's bad day at school has affected an entire group of children and adults. The living group is dynamic, constantly changing. Care workers need to continually observe the constant changes in the mood and balance of the group in order to maintain a healthy group that provides a safe, relaxed, and caring atmosphere.

The literature abounds with models of how groups develop (Braaten, Dunphy, LaCoursiere, Mann, Miles, Spitz, Tuckman & Jensen, Yalom, Zurcher). Theories of group development have as few as three and as many as 12 phases that groups go through as they develop. In care settings, the living groups go through stages of development. This progression is not smooth since every time a child or staff member joins or leaves the group, the group, in a sense, goes back to the beginning. Because of the transitory nature of group care, it might be most useful for care workers to focus their efforts and skills on group inclusion, group purpose, and group norms, and taking advantage of everyday interactions as an opportunity to improve children's interpersonal skills (Brendtro & Ness, 1983; Echternacht, 2001). By focusing on establishing pro-social group norms, helping new children and staff belong to the group, and teaching children interpersonal skills, the group can withstand the constant changes and maintain a sense of purpose and cohesion.

All theories of group development agree that there is a beginning phase. This phase is when the group is forming and members are either included or excluded. Children and young people have very little say, if any, as to what group they will join when they are placed in group care. It is a forced living situation and may result in the child feeling powerless and vulnerable. Just as children have had trouble attaching to adults, their experiences in belonging to peer groups most likely have been weighed down with difficulties and damaging experiences. Previously, inclusion or claiming was presented as a way to help children form attachments. In group care, becoming *one of us*, part of the group, is based on sharing experiences. Children get up at the same time, eat together, go to school together, do chores together, participate in activities together, celebrate events, and so on. These common experiences provide a basis for developing a sense of belonging and feeling a part of something. It is important for children and young people to belong to their living group and be claimed by their living group. Care workers are instrumental in orchestrating the development of *groupness* and ensuring that all children have the sense of belonging to the living group by successfully participating in daily events.

It is common practice in group care, classrooms, or other settings that work with groups of children to exclude children from the group or activity if they exhibit behavioral difficulties. These strategies are often called *time out* or *chill time*. Care workers need to carefully assess the use of these types of excluding strategies since the child loses the opportunity to attach to the group and develop the interpersonal skills necessary to function in a group setting. The more skilled care workers are at using these moments for teaching skills, the more skilled the children become at being part of a group.

Group Purpose

Groups tend to be more effective and functional if there is a clear purpose or goal for the group (Brendtro & Ness, 1983; Johnson & Johnson, 1975; Malekoff, 1997). The purpose of the organization is usually presented as a mission or vision and written in agency documentation. The children and young people also need to have this expressed in ways that make sense to them. Working this out *in* partnership rather than presenting it *to* them has enormous benefits. This statement of purpose needs to be embedded in daily living activities so that both staff and youth know it and respect it. Activities and interactions that take place in the group need to be consciously designed to support the purpose. All the activities of daily life and living need to lead to the purpose of the living group and to meeting needs of the individuals within the group. This helps to keep the children and young people focused. For example, if *the purpose of this group is to help everyone who is a part of the group to improve their behavior and manage their anger*, when the group gets off track and behavior becomes belligerent, aggressive, or out of control, staff can work with the group to help bring them back to the purpose of the group. Having a stated, acknowledged, agreed upon purpose helps staff and children concentrate on why they are there and what needs to be accomplished to achieve the goals.

Group goals and purpose are more effective if they take into consideration the world-view and cultural diversity of the group and the individual members' goals (Group Child Care Consultants, 1977; Johnson & Johnson, 1975; Ward, 2004). Even though it is a group, a group is made up of individuals. If children fear the group may not meet their personal needs, they may disrupt the group. When children know that the purpose and goal of the group includes what they need and hope for, they are more likely to relax and trust the group process.

Group Norms

If a group is going to be cohesive and work together, there must be group norms. Group norms are values and beliefs the group members have about how they are expected to behave and interact with each other. The living group will have different norms than the school group. These norms may be formal or informal, spoken about openly, or unspoken. They are powerful and have tremendous influence on the group's behavior. If someone violates a group norm, spoken or unspoken, the group may react with hostility (Abrams, Rutland, & Cameron, 2003). For example, if the group norm is to allow a child to have privacy when upset and talking to a care worker and another group member interferes with the conversation, the group may turn on the one who is interfering.

As children enter school and adolescence, peer relationships and peer group influence also have a role in developing pro-social skills (Harris, 1998, 2006). If the norm within the peer group is to follow rules and use pro-social skills, children will usually fit in by exhibiting the same behavior. When it is difficult for the child to adhere to the norm, peers can be supportive and help the child develop the skills.

Care workers can help the group develop positive, socially acceptable norms by assisting the group to bring the norms out into the open and make a conscious decision to accept or reject the norm. Establishing norms through group discussion is usually the most effective way to develop them, acknowledge they exist, and agree to them. Norms will most likely be accepted if they help achieve the group goals. Cooperation in developing these norms promotes a sense of belonging as all members work together to achieve a common purpose (Beck & Malley, 1998). Norms supporting physical and emotional safety, growth and change, mutual support and helping others, open communication, individuality, cultural diversity, and privacy should be encouraged. Children are also more likely to accept norms if they have helped set them up and see other group members abide by them. When members of the group violate the norms of the group, they should immediately be challenged and helped to get back on track.

Group Management

As discussed earlier, the mix of the group has consequences for how the group works and lives together. The care worker's job is not to control the group but to work with and within group process to help young people individually and collectively achieve developmental and individual goals.

There is a link between a democratic leadership style and effective group management (Hubble et al., 1999). Respecting young people and expecting them to act responsibly, encouraging and teaching youth to solve their own problems, and actively involving youth in discussions and decisions are part of a democratic leadership style (Kohn, 1999; Nelson, 1996; Stewart, 2002). Young people in group care have the ability to help each other, with adult assistance (Emond, 2002, 2003; Vorrath & Brendtro, 1985). As children work together toward a common goal, they become a community whose members care about each other and are committed to each other's welfare, and who can achieve more than if they were working alone (Berman, 1997; Fawcett & Garton, 2005). Young people in group care can identify and rely on other youth to assist them when they need help.

Different young people are valued by other youth based on their personal strengths and competencies. Although groups will tend to have leaders and followers, this does not have to be a rigid structure. It can be much more fluid, with status based on what the young people contribute as different needs arise. Care workers can assist in this process by helping group members identify strengths and encourage young people to help each other. Activities can be structured so that all individuals have a chance to take a leadership role emphasizing their strengths and interests. The more care workers can do to help group members understand and appreciate each other's strengths and needs the less likely groups will be to fall apart and be riddled with scapegoats, negative leaders, and gang mentalities.

Skills that care workers need to accomplish these tasks are the same skills necessary to form attachments, build relationships, and teach self-regulation skills. Care workers need to be able to observe behavior, listen to what the youth are saying, communicate their understanding, give choices, facilitate discussions, set limits, and problem-solve.

Group Problem-Solving

When problems occur among the children that affect how they are living, working, and playing together, group problem-solving may be the best intervention strategy. Allowing children the opportunity to work together, to communicate their feelings and goals, listen to each other, and then collaborate to find a solution that everyone can embrace, is a way to strengthen group identity, increase children's abilities to communicate and problem-solve, and reaffirm the norms of how everyone wants to live together.

Care workers can encourage and manage this process by:

(1)   Helping the children establish group norms for solving problems. The care worker can then reinforce these norms when the discussion or atmosphere is tense.

(2)   Ensuring that all children express their feelings and needs and listen and understand each other's perspective.

(3)   Assisting the children and young people in discussing alternatives to solve the problem.

(4)   Guiding the children in making a decision that all can live with and abide by.

(5)   Observing how the solution is working (or not), and celebrating its effectiveness or encouraging the group to come back together and find a more suitable solution.

The more the children and young people are involved in making decisions about what they are going to do, how they are going to live together, and how they share power with each other and the care workers, the more they will feel in control of their lives. Care workers must be confident and skilled in their ability to facilitate these processes and they must be willing to let go of their *power* in order to become more influential. When care workers assist children and young people to take responsibility for their lives, life skills are taught, power struggles are reduced, and the quality of life is improved for everyone who lives and works there. ✿

CHAPTER 22

Learning Life Skills Through Activity Programming

Play is the child's work.
—*Marie Montessori*

Play is fundamental to children and young people as they naturally strive for mastery and competence in meeting life's demands. Children play with dolls and care for pets as a way to learn how to be responsible and care for others. Playing house, dressing up, building forts, baking cookies, erecting tents, and making campfires are preparation for adult life. Sports and games develop physical skills, teach children relationship skills, and teach children how to cooperate and work together.

Art and music are outlets for creative energy and emotional turmoil. Drama and fantasy play help children and youth work through past traumatic events and cope with emotional stress. Hobbies and activities build on strengths and interests, helping children develop a sense of identity. Leisure time activities teach children how to have fun and enjoy life in a healthy, positive way. Yet many residential programs are activity poor and limit activities to the children who have earned them (Mohr et al., 2009; VanderVen, 2005).

Work and Service To Others

Work projects, chores, taking care of others, running errands, or assisting a teacher, staff, or other child help children develop a sense of personal investment, accomplishment, and pride in a job well done. Being asked to share generously of one's time and efforts helps promote moral development and allows children to see beyond what is in the best interests of *me*. They begin to see themselves as useful to others and valuable. Asking everyone to contribute to the well-being of the community helps build a sense of self-worth, as well as teaches children how to care for others. Sharing in the community also develops a sense of responsibility and teaches children how to follow directions. Yet many residential programs assign meaningless tasks to children or, even worse, use work and/or community service as a punishment for inappropriate behavior.

Play, a Necessary Developmental Activity

In the literature, play is well established as a necessary activity for normal growth and development of physical, cognitive, and interpersonal skills (Bettelheim, 1950; Cole, 1996; Erikson, 1963; Freud, 1965; Greenspan, 1999; Montessori, 1912; Piaget, 1951; VanderVen, 1999; Vygotsky, 1978). Play is also an important tool in helping children work through traumatic experiences (Bloom, 1997; Garbarino, 1995; Garbarino, Dubrow, Kostelny, & Pardo, 1992; Perry, 2002a). Play is the main avenue for learning, exploring, and interacting. It allows children and youth the opportunity to risk learning from trial and error, to win and lose, and to try things that are scary without permanent or terrible repercussions. It is the essence of experiential learning. Play also provides for stress reduction and release of emotions in a safe and appropriate manner. Most importantly, play is fun! Many children and youth in care have had their childhood stolen. Their histories reflect how they have had to deal with adult issues as children, often resulting in missed opportunities to delight in discovery and free play promoting creativity and flexibility.

Additionally, activities may serve as practice ground for reaching out, having fun, or serious exchange with peers of the opposite sex. All of these capabilities have to be learned and are vital benchmarks on the path to greater self-worth and maturity and, eventually, to young adulthood (Alwon, 1979; Holden & Holden, 1990).

Play and Work As a Relationship Tool

In addition to the opportunity to learn important life skills, play and work afford care workers the opportunity to engage with the children in relationship-building activities. Simultaneous involvement in an activity, be it work or play, allows the adult and child to connect with each other in a more neutral and relaxed environment. Sharing ideas and interests creates a personal context for relating to each other and adds another layer to the relationship. Staff members can offer special activities and contribute to the team and serve as role models for developing interests, skills, and the discipline associated with an activity (Mohr et al., 2009; VanderVen, 2005). When the care worker engages fully and enthusiastically in the activity with the young person instead of supervising from a distance, not only is the relationship strengthened, the activity is more successful.

Involving families in activities provides a means to develop relationships with family members, encourage a partnership between the family and child, and model a variety of ways to engage in fun and productive activities. Family members can relax and participate in the community of the residential agency in a nonthreatening atmosphere. Children can demonstrate their strengths and newly developed skills and friendships. Families can contribute ideas and resources to activity events highlighting their talents, interests, and abilities and sharing their own cultural background.

Planning Successful Activities

What is the key to successful activities? Planning is critical and includes setting a goal; choosing an activity based on the goal; understanding the abilities, motivations, and self-regulation skills of the group and individuals; securing adequate resources and space; and possessing a good sense of timing (Brendtro & Ness, 1983; Krueger, 1983, 2007; Mayer, 1978; Trieschman et al., 1969; VanderVen, 2005; Ward, 2004).

Setting Goals

All activities should be purposeful, even if the primary purpose is to have fun and *let off steam*. Is the activity designed to enhance physical coordination and strength; increase communication skills; develop problem-solving or conflict resolution skills; promote self-control and management of emotions; improve relationships and group cohesion; instill values of caring, service, and generosity; create good work habits; or encourage creativity and free play? Planning should occur in advance, even if one is planning for spontaneity.

Once the goal has been established, care workers can assess the children's progress, guide the play and interaction, and process the event with the group, individual, and team. Again, if the sole purpose was to have fun, asking the questions, "Was it fun?" and "What made it fun?" help recognize that it was successful and what contributed to that success. The effectiveness of group activities can be assessed by how well the goal was achieved. When goals are achieved, the group can celebrate its success. If goals are not achieved, it is an opportunity to learn from the experience, plan a different strategy, and try again.

Able, Willing, and Ready

It is important to consider the individual and group readiness to participate in the activity. Do the children and young people have the skills to participate successfully with adult support? What is the motivational level or willingness of the young people? The more complex the activity, the more motivation the children will have to have to complete it. Are they emotionally ready to handle any frustrations or excitement that might be generated through the activity? Are care workers capable and ready to deal with children's frustrations and excitement generated in the activities?

As important as it is to learn to win and lose, succeed and fail, and overcome barriers and frustrations, children must be prepared to handle these stressful situations. Activities may need to be adjusted or individual children may need additional supports to participate successfully in the activity.

Resources

Before announcing the activity, it is important to have the equipment, space, and materials ready to start. Many an activity has been sabotaged because children lost interest by the time the materials were found and made ready, or not found at all. This is as true for work activities as it is for play. Equally necessary is adequate space to freely conduct the activity. Participants in the activity should not be concerned about breaking things or running into walls or out into the street. There are a variety of valuable resources for games, experiential learning, and group problem-solving activities, and care workers should use them. These resources are available at any library or bookstore.

Timing Is Everything

Knowing when to start a song, tell a story, toss a ball, or clean a closet is a matter of good timing. These spontaneous activities are important to children and young people as they derive a lot of pleasure from these relaxed, intimate moments. Care workers who have the ability to know when and how to engage children in the spur of the moment are valuable assets to any program. Although these events appear and feel spontaneous, the care worker had to have these activities in mind and waited for the right moment to introduce them.

Just as important as knowing when to start an activity, is knowing when to stop it. Many a game or project has started out with everyone enthusiastically participating, only to be ended with threats of punishment if the children do not *finish what they started*. An opportunity for a successful, satisfying, reinforcing experience has ended in frustration, bad feelings, and inappropriate behavior. A care worker has to read the mood and tolerance of the group and know when to end an activity. A good metric is to end the game when it is at or near the peak of having the most fun, leaving them wanting more. This gives care workers a sure winner the next time they need a game!

Summary

Being part of a group is a basic, healthy, and normal activity for people from childhood to old age. Having a sense of belonging in a group that is guided by constructive values may be a new and positive experience for many children who have come into care having only experienced negative peer influence. A positive group experience does not just happen; care workers have a large role in forming the group and maintaining it through various shifts and changes. Having a purpose and clear goals for the group will help to bring the group together in pursuit of a common goal, while having group norms gives group members a code of conduct to follow and obey. Assisting the group in problem-solving teaches the children in the group to work together, and communicate, and strengthens the group. A care worker is a guide and mediator in this process, and good guidance is the surest way to a successful group.

Participation in work and service opportunities teaches children responsibility and investment in the community; play aids social, physical, and cognitive development; both activities provide opportunities for care workers to build relationships with children. Activities must have a purpose, must take into account the abilities of all participants, must be possible given the resources available, and must be timed correctly and appropriately. When activities work, they can be valuable tools to help children and groups reach goals, and can strengthen relationships between workers and the children in their care. ✿

ESSENTIAL CONNECTIONS

CHAPTER 23

Building Essential Connections

There are only two lasting bequests we can hope to give our children. One is roots, the other, wings.

—Hodding Carter

When helping children develop life skills necessary for a healthy, satisfying life, all of the principles of this course come together. The quality of life is dependent on how one interacts with one's environment, how well the individual has overcome past traumatic events and managed developmental tasks, the level of competence one has achieved, and how supporting and caring the relationships in one's life are, especially the ties to family. For human beings to have successful interactions in their environment, they need nine essential attachments or connections to meet their needs and manage most of life's situations (Hansell, 1976; Pasztor, Polowy, Wasson & Wolf, 1987) (see Table 8). These connections are interdependent; they are related to each other. If any one of these attachments remains disconnected for any period of time, it erodes the other attachments. Identifying young people's lack of connections and negative connections and then working to build attachments and life skills to maintain these attachments will help them lead productive lives.

TABLE 8. ESSENTIAL CONNECTIONS

Information/Knowledge	What we need to know in order to live in the world.
Identity	Knowing who we are by understanding where we come from.
Significant Person	A person who is important in our lives.
Group	People with whom we associate and feel like we belong.
Meaningful Role	What we do that gives meaning to our lives.
Means of Support	The way we support ourselves and our family.
Source of Joy	The things that make us happy.
System of Values and Meaning	What we believe in that drives our decisionmaking.
Place	The places or spaces where we feel at home.

Information and Knowledge

What knowledge is necessary to live in the world? This is the most basic and most abstract of the attachments. It is as basic as where a person must go to get food and water, and as complex as what a person needs to know to be successful in the world. When people are cut off from the flow of information, apathy often sets in. Without access to information, young people may have unrealistic fantasies about family and future; they may be unmotivated to learn life skills or complete their education due to a lack of understanding of personal needs. When people have control of the information flow, they exhibit a healthy sense of curiosity and seeking of new and needed information. Children and young people will need a lot of information and knowledge to lead interdependent adult lives.

Identity

Much has already been discussed about the importance of identity and self-efficacy. Since children and adolescents are in the process of developing their own identity separate from their families, much of who they are is attached to their history and their life experiences (Bandura, 1994; Erikson, 1963). Family, culture, race, and experiences come together to help children and young people develop a strong identity. Being separated from family and culture without a strong sense of self can result in a lack of clarity or conviction about who they are and where they are going in life. They may fail to understand past life events and be stuck dealing with unresolved issues, unable to move on. Helping to understand the past can free a person up to plan and work for the future.

Significant Person

As Urie Bronfenbrenner, one of the world's leading scholars in the field of developmental psychology, is often quoted, "Every child needs at least one person who is really crazy about him." Everyone needs someone in their life who cares about them and for whom they care. This is the most essential attachment and is important for developing the capacity of intimacy, trust, and self-worth (Bowlby, 1970; Fahlberg, 1991). Without a significant other, youth may feel unloved and unlovable, resulting in a poor self-concept. They are less likely to trust and may be unwilling to learn new behaviors. Helping children attach or reattach to healthy adults can provide the stability and support they need to make it in life.

Group

Everyone requires at least one group attachment to assist with food, shelter, and recreation and to help through periods of stress and upset. For most children this group begins with family. As children grow, they begin to attach to groups based on interest and the need to belong and develop an identity (Bowlby, 1970; Brendtro et al., 1998; Fahlberg, 1991; Maslow, 1987). Without a connection to a group, children may have increased feelings of isolation and an inability to negotiate within the social environment. They will also struggle with developing an identity since this involves being connected to a group.

In care, children may attach and identify with the living group. As they progress toward discharge, helping children find positive groups in the community will provide them with support and opportunities to share interests.

Meaningful Role

Leading a purposeful life is tied into feelings of self-worth and dignity (Brendtro et al., 1998). People need to demonstrate to others that they can accomplish a task, contribute to society, and are of value to others. This directly relates to a young person's ability to be and feel competent and worthwhile. Without a meaningful role, children may feel incompetent and unable to contribute. Feelings of inadequacy and low self-worth will reduce the motivation to work and to look toward the future with optimism. Community service projects, assisting others in the group, and giving something of oneself to others in need, are all ways to help children feel competent and worthwhile.

Means of Support

This is exactly what it says—a way to earn money or obtain goods and services to survive. This usually implies a job or some way to earn money, be part of the economic system, and obtain a standard of living. Being disconnected from this attachment usually results in poverty. Poverty denotes much more than insufficient funds; it includes gaps in access to health and educational services. If children come from a family that was disconnected from the economy structure, they may be ill-equipped to connect themselves to this important attachment (Hansell, 1976). Teaching valuable, necessary skills to compete in the economy and support oneself in the future is an important part of residential care.

A System of Values and Meaning

This system encompasses the beliefs and values that guide a person's decisions throughout life and help define what is proper and ethical. It involves the spiritual development of the human capacity for self-transcendence, the knowledge that there is something greater than self which propels a sense of connection, meaning, purpose, and contribution (Benson, Roehlkepartain & Rude, 2003). This can be described as religion, lifestyle, ethics, spirituality, or common sense. It is the map by which a person travels through life. Spiritual anchors lead to a sense of purpose, to meaningfulness, and to future orientation (Coles, 1990; Garbarino, 1999). When disconnected from a value system, all choices are equal and confusion over what is right and what is forbidden may paralyze a person's capacity for making decisions. If all choices are equal, young people may engage in socially unacceptable behaviors because they are the easier path or will quickly satisfy a need. Programs will do well to build in time for reflection, contemplation, and meditation, providing character education and conversations around moral reasoning. Supporting spiritual development activities will aid children in developing a value system. Avoiding power tactics and creating a nonviolent, peaceful culture throughout the organization will assist these efforts.

Source of Joy

Everyone needs opportunities to experience happiness and joy. What events, activities, people, rituals give pleasure? Joy is sometimes a product of a system of values. The need to relax, reduce stress and tension, have fun and play are met through a variety of sources of joy. Without sources of joy, children may become depressed, isolated, and lose their sense of belonging and connectedness to the world. There will be less meaning in the child's life and their behavior and motivation will suffer. Programs that involve children in a range of activities and emphasize the fun that people can have sharing these experiences will help children find their own sources of joy.

Place

Everyone needs a home, a place in the world that has special, personal meaning. *Where are you from?* is a question that often begins a social interaction. Life experiences with friends, family, and neighborhoods are associated with places. The need for shelter and security, personal space, and privacy are all attached to special spaces (Maier, 1987; Maslow, 1987). Without this connection, children may feel insecure and rootless. Helping children identify spaces where they feel safe and secure in the residential center, as well as in the community, will help them transition out of placement.

Building Positive Connections

Children and young people come into care with many of these connections severed or with connections that are harmful. Once they are placed in care, many additional connections are lost. Sometimes the very rules or location of an organization separate children from their attachments. With each severed connection, there are resultant feelings and behaviors that children express to give care workers clues as to the loss the child is experiencing. While in care, staff members may work to separate youth from harmful or negative connections (such as a gang [group], drugs [joy], stealing [means of support]). With so many connections lost, young people will fight to keep what connections they have. Instead of immediately shutting down these negative connections, it might be easier to try to build more positive connections in other areas and then replace the negative connections with positive ones. By careful observation and talking with the young people, care workers and the team can assist children and young people in reclaiming or rebuilding their connections and establishing positive connections. This work takes careful planning, involvement, and decisionmaking with the young person and coordination by the team. It is the care worker and team's responsibility and duty to try to build and reconnect these attachments so that the children have the promise of a better life when they return to the community.

Summary

Life is about making essential connections to one's environment, peers, and protectors. Nine essential connections have been identified as critical to the healthy development of all human beings. (1) Information and knowledge are what a person needs to know to be successful in the world. (2) Identity is one's self-efficacy and helps children work toward the future with the belief that they can succeed. (3) Having a significant person who cares develops one's capacity for intimacy, trust, and self-worth. (4) Being part of a group gives a sense of belonging and provides a support network. (5) Having a meaningful role gives purpose in life. (6) A means of support is necessary to avoid poverty and provide for oneself and family. (7) A system of values and meaning helps one make the right choices and provides a map to travel through life. (8) A source of joy provides opportunities to relax and be happy. (9) Connection to a place is one's roots. Many essential connections may have been missing from a child's life when the child came into care and those they do possess may be negative. It is the all-encompassing job of the care worker, the group, and the organization to provide as many opportunities for positive connections as possible. ✿

THE STRUGGLE FOR CONGRUENCE IN THE BEST INTERESTS OF THE CHILD

CHAPTER 24
Team Work and the Struggle for Congruence

Never doubt that a small group of thoughtful, committed citizens can change the world. Indeed, it is the only thing that ever has.

—*Margaret Mead*

In residential care, no one can be truly effective working in isolation. The best interests of the children can only be achieved through collective effort and cooperation. Because it is an interconnected system, the way members of an organization interact and behave with one another is reflected in the way they interact and behave with the children and their families. As stated previously, one of the core challenges for residential group care organizations is to achieve congruence throughout the agency in serving the best interests of the children who reside there (Anglin, 2002). This struggle for congruence is nowhere more apparent than in the ongoing decisionmaking and planning process at the team level. There are always competing interests, including resources, children's needs, family needs, staff needs, regulations, and placing agencies' demands. Balancing these separate demands and placing the children's needs above all other interests is a struggle. Making decisions that are in the best interest of the children takes constant work and diligence to keep the process a positive and open one, focused on the organization's mission and the principles that underpin the way children and families are to be served. In healthy groups, teams, and systems, everyone collaborates in a climate of open communication, collaborative problem-solving, mutual support and respect, and accountability for individual and group actions.

What Is a Residential Care Team?

Team in its simplest form in residential care is a "group of people with individual expertise, skill, knowledge and responsibility for the planning, decision making, and the provision of treatment (care) for children" (M. J. Holden, 1983) in their care. What takes place in a therapeutic milieu is generally in the hands of the treatment team and the care workers. The many roles involved in a treatment team include, but are not limited to, direct care workers, teachers, therapists, recreation specialists, supervisors, nurses, and perhaps the most important members of the team— the children and their families.

One way to consider a team is by viewing the team as a system whereby each member affects each other member of the team in some way. How effective one member is in carrying out his or her role has an effect on other members of the team and ultimately the effectiveness of the team (Krueger et al., 1999). For example, if one member of the team is habitually late to work, the following may occur:

- because the staff person is late, the morning program has to be adjusted;
- other care workers may become frustrated because they have to pick up the slack;
- teachers may become irritated since they have to change a schedule because they need all children present for an activity and the child was late because of staff shortage;

- the nurse is now running behind because of the house schedule change;
- the supervisor was to meet with the care worker but now has to adjust his or her schedule; or
- a youth who has developed a relationship with the staff begins to question in her mind whether the staff really cares for her.

This simplistic example shows a domino effect that one member may have on the other members of the team.

One could say that most of our clients are victims of poor team work prior to their referral for service, poor team work between parents, poor teamwork between parents and school systems, poor teamwork between parents and social service and mental health agencies (Alwon, 2000).

It is incumbent upon team members to continuously strive for the most effective working relationship possible in the best interests of the child and family, and to do this through reflective practice.

Team Member Roles

Defining roles in a team is a very complex issue since some roles are very specific, such as *who is responsible for getting children off to school in the morning* to the more general, *who is responsible for diffusing a potential crisis situation* and *who is responsible for helping youth meet their treatment goals*. Effective teams are best served through the development and understanding of clear and specific roles for each of the team members. That specificity allows for individual members to draw upon individual strengths and expertise in planning and decisionmaking.

The fundamental asset the care worker has is himself/herself. Self-awareness, self-regulation, self-motivation, empathy, and social skills, in addition to ethnic and multicultural competence, are the fundamental attributes a care worker needs to bring to the team. Care workers are potentially the most significant adults in the residential experience for the child. The primary role of the care worker is to develop and maintain relationships with the children and young people in their care (Fahlberg, 1990; Maier, 1987). Team decisions, assignments, and professional development activities should reflect that priority.

Establishing Goals

Ultimately, the collective team members are drawn together with a common goal of serving the best interest of the child and the child's family. In addition, the team will develop additional short- and long-term goals. Goals are motivating forces for groups and keep members committed to immediate tasks. Just as discussed when examining the living groups, motivation is increased when the members participate in setting the goals. Everyone has individual goals for their own professional growth and development. The more relevant team goals are to achievement of personal goals, the better the functioning of the group. The more oriented the team is toward cooperative behavior and collaborative decisionmaking and problem-solving, the better the commitment to the team goals (Johnson & Johnson, 1975).

Communication

Communication, verbal and written, formal and informal, is the vehicle through which team members interact and work together. Open and ongoing communication is absolutely necessary and time-consuming. Schedules must be coordinated so all members can meet together. Record keeping must be accurate, timely, and contain information that is useful and all team members must have good written and verbal communication skills. Individual team members must be willing to share feelings, ideas, and personal goals clearly. Positive and corrective feedback should be an expected and desired part of the communication process. Working with traumatized and troubled children through a relationship-based practice approach is a demanding way of working. When teams adopt reflective practice principles and provide a collaborative and communicative way of working, such as informal and formal discussions and regular consultation sessions, care workers are much more able to be self-aware and effectively respond to and survive the emotionally charged nature of the work (Ruch, 2005). Teams will also need to work, develop, and maintain an effective way of communicating, decisionmaking, planning, and problem-solving through continual staff development and team-building activities.

Striving for Excellence in the Best Interests of the Children

The team and organization's ability to provide an environment in which children can thrive is dependent on the quality of the milieu. The care workers' skills and motivation to respond appropriately and therapeutically to children's pain-based behavior is dependent on training and supervision. The team's capacity to prepare children for a healthy future by helping to normalize their experiences and promote socially acceptable behaviors is in the hands of the organization's leadership. Dedication to the organization's mission, values, and guiding principles that serve the best interests of the children and their families is essential. Inspiring commitment at all levels of the organization, providing the necessary resources, and sharing power and decisionmaking are tools that leadership will need to use to develop and maintain services that meet the needs of the children, families, staff members, and teams. By keeping the guiding principles outlined in the course (developmentally focused, family-involved, relationship-based, competence-centered, trauma-informed, and ecologically oriented) in the forefront of discussions and decisions and resource allocation, organizations can provide quality, best practices care and treatment to children and young people in their care. This is truly in the best interests of the children.

Summary

Working with children in care is not an individual effort, but the efforts of a team that includes not only the care workers and other staff, but also the families and the children themselves. It is important that each member of the team know their role in the treatment process, establish goals collaboratively, and, above all, communicate effectively with one another. The goal for all residential settings should be service in the best interests of the child. With that goal kept in mind by all who have a role in a child's treatment and care, and a working knowledge of the principles of good care, workers can make the right decisions with the children in their care. ✿

References &
Additional Resources

References

Abramovitz, R., & Bloom, S. (2003). Creating sanctuary in residential treatment for youth: From the "well-ordered asylum" to a "living learning environment." *Psychiatric Quarterly, 74*(2), 119-135.

Abrams, D., Rutland, A., & Cameron, L. (2003). The development of subjective group dynamics: Children's judgments of normative and deviant in-group and out-group individuals. *Child Development, 74*(6), 1840-1856.

Aichorn, A. (1925). *Wayward youth.* New York: The Viking Press.

Ainsworth, F. (1999). Place as a source of attachment and identity across the life course. *Journal of Child and Youth Care Work, 13*(2), 58-67.

Ainsworth, M. (1967). *Infancy in Uganda: Infant care and the growth of love.* Baltimore: Johns Hopkins University Press.

Alwon, F. J. (1979). An after school activity club program. *Child Care Quarterly, 8*(4), 266-278.

Alwon, F. (2000). *Effective supervisory practice.* Washington, DC: Child Welfare League of America.

Alwon, F., Budlong, M., Holden, J., Holden, M., Kuhn, F., Mooney, A., et al. (1988). *Connecting: Essential elements of residential child care practice.* Atlanta, GA: Child Welfare Institute.

Amulya, J. (2004). *What is reflective practice?* Boston: The Center for Reflective Community Practice at MIT.

Anglin, J. (2002). *Pain, normality, and the struggle for congruence.* New York: The Haworth Press, Inc.

Arnold, M. E., & Hughes, J. N. (1999). First do no harm; adverse effects of grouping deviant youth for skills training. *Journal of School Psychology, 37*(1), 99-115.

Balbernie, R. (1972). *Residential work with children.* London: Human Context Books.

Bandura, A. (1994). Self-efficacy. In V. S. Ramachaudran, (Ed.), *Encyclopedia of human behavior* (Vol. 4, pp. 71-81). New

York: Academic Press. (Reprinted in H. Friedman [Ed.], *Encyclopedia of mental health*. San Diego: Academic Press, 1998).

Bandura, A. (1997). *Self-efficacy: The exercise of control.* New York: Worth Publishers.

Barth, R. P. (2005). Residential care: From here to eternity. *International Journal of Social Work, 14,* 158-162.

Barth, R. P., Greeson, J. K. P., Guo, S., Green, R. L, Hurley, S., & Sisson, J. (2007). Outcomes for youth receiving intensive in-home therapy or residential care: A comparison using propensity scores. *American Journal of Orthopsychiatry, 77*(4), 497-505.

Bath, H. (2008). Calming together: The pathway to self-control. *Reclaiming Children and Youth, 15*(4), 44-49.

Beck, M., & Malley, J. (1998). A pedagogy of belonging. *Reclaiming Children and Youth, 7*(3), 133-137.

Belknap, N. (2001). Minding the children in 1951: Who is minding them in 2001? *Reclaiming Children and Youth, 10*(2), 66-70.

Benard, B. (1991). *Fostering resiliency in kids: Protective factors within the family, school, and community.* Portland, OR: Northwest Regional Educational Laboratory.

Benard, B. (2004). *Resiliency: What we have learned.* San Francisco: West Ed.

Benson, P., Roehlkepartain, E., & Rude, S. (2003). Spiritual development in childhood and adolescence: Toward a field of inquiry. *Applied Developmental Science, 7*(3), 205-213.

Berman, S. (1997). *Children's social consciousness and the development of social responsibility.* Albany, NY: State University of New York Press.

Bettelheim, B. (1950). *Love is not enough.* New York: Free Press.

Bettelheim, B. (1974). *A home for the heart.* New York: Knopf.

Bloom, S. (1997). *Creating sanctuary: Toward the evolution of sane societies.* New York: Routledge.

Bowlby, J. (1970). *Attachment and loss. Volume I Attachment.* New York: Basic Books.

Brendtro, L. (1990). Powerful pioneers in residential group care. *Child and Youth Care Quarterly, 19*(2).

Brendtro, L. (2004). *From coercive to strength-based intervention: Responding to the needs of children in pain.* Conference paper. Copyright: No Disposable Kids, Inc.

Brendtro, L., Brokenleg, M., & Van Bockern, S. (1998). *Reclaiming youth at risk: Our hope for the future.* Bloomington IN: National Education Service.

Brendtro, L., & Shahbazian, M. (2004). *Troubled children and youth: Turning problems into opportunities.* Champaign, IL: Research Press.

Brendtro, L., & Ness, A. (1983). *Re-educating troubled youth: Environments for teaching and treatments.* Hawthorne, NY: Aldine.

Bronfenbrenner, U. (1979). *The ecology of human development.* Cambridge, MA: Harvard University Press.

Cicchetti, D., & Tucker, D. (1994). Development and self-regulatory structures of the mind. *Development and Psychopathology, 6*, 533–549.

Cohler, B., & Zimmerman, D. (2000). Youth in residential care: From war nursery to therapeutic milieu. *Residential Treatment for Children & Youth, 18*(2), 1-25.

Cole, M. (1996). *Cultural psychology: A once and future discipline.* Cambridge, MA: Harvard University Press.

Curry, J. (1991). Outcome research on residential treatment: Implications and suggested directions. *American Journal of Orthopsychiatry, 61*, 348-358.

de Schipper, E. F., Riksen-Walraven, J. M., Geurts, S. A. E., & Derksen, J. J. L. (2008). General mood of professional caregivers in child care centers and the quality of caregiver-child interactions. *Journal of Research in Personality, 42,* 515-526.

Dockar-Drysdale, B. (1968). *Therapy in child care.* London: Longman.

Echternacht, M. (2001). Fluid group: Concept and clinical application in the therapeutic milieu. *Journal of the American Psychiatric Nurses Association, 7*(2), 39-44.

Egan, G. (2002). *The skilled helper: A problem-management and opportunity-development approach to helping.* Pacific Grove, CA: Brooks/Cole, Thompson Learning, Inc.

Eisikovits, Z., & Beker, J. E. (1991). The known and used in residential child and youth care work. In J. E. Beker & Z. Eisikovitz (Eds.), *Knowledge utilization in residential child and youth care work.* Washington, DC: Child Welfare League of America.

Elkind, D., & Weiner, I. (1978). *Development of the child.* New York: Wiley Publishers.

Emond, R. (2002). Understanding the resident group. *Scottish Journal of Residential Child Care,* (1), 30-39.

Emond, R. (2003). Putting the care into residential care: The role of young people. *Journal of Social Work, 3*(3), 321-377.

Erikson, E. H. (1950). *Childhood and society.* New York: Norton.

Erikson, E.H. (1963). *Childhood and society (2nd ed.).* New York: Norton.

Fahlberg, V. (1990). *Residential treatment: A tapestry of many therapies.* Indianapolis, IN: Perspectives Press.

Fahlberg, V. (1991). *A child's journey through placement.* Indianapolis, IN: Perspectives Press.

Fanshel, D., & Shinn, E. B. (1978). *Children in foster care: A longitudinal investigation.* New York: Columbia University Press.

Farmer, E., & Pollock, S. (1999). Mix and match: Planning to keep looked after children safe. *Child Abuse Review, 8*, 377-391.

Fawcett, L., & Garton, A. (2005). The effect of peer collaboration on children's problem-solving ability. *British Journal of Educational Psychology, 75*, 157-169.

Feldman, S., & Elliott, G. (Eds.). (1990). *At the threshold: The developing adolescent.* Cambridge, MA: Harvard University Press, 1-13.

Fewster, G. (1990b). *Perspectives in professional child and youth care.* Binghamton, NY: The Haworth Press, Inc.

Freud, A. (1965). *The concept of developmental lines. The writings of Anna Freud.* (Vol. 6). Madison, CT: International Universities Press.

Fulcher, L., & Ainsworth, F. (2006). *Group care for children and young people revisited.* New York: Haworth Press.

Garbarino, J. (1995). *Raising children in a socially toxic environment.* San Francisco: Jossey-Bass.

Garbarino, J. (1999). *Lost boys: Why our sons turn violent and how we can save them.* New York: The Free Press.

Garbarino, J., Dubrow, N., Kostelny, K., & Pardo, C. (1992). *Children in danger: Coping with the consequences of community violence.* San Francisco: Jossey-Bass.

Garbarino, J., & Holden, M. (1997). *Let's talk about living in a world with violence.* Ithaca, NY: Cornell University.

Gardner, T. W., Dishion, T. J., & Connell, A. M. (2008). Adolescent self-regulation as resiliency: Resistance to antisocial behavior within the deviant peer context. *Journal of Abnormal Child Psychology, 36*, 273-284.

Garfat, T. (2004). *A child and youth care approach to working with families.* New York: Haworth Press.

Gerhardt, S. (2004). *Why love matters: How affection shapes a baby's brain.* New York: Routledge.

Germain, C., & Gitterman, A. (1996). *The life model of social work practice. (2nd ed.).* New York: Columbia University Press.

Gestsdottir, S., & Lerner, R. M. (2008). Positive development in adolescence: The development and role of intentional self-regulation. *Human Development, 51,* 202-224.

Gibson, J. (2003). Anger: Troublesome emotion or therapeutic challenge? *Refocus, 8,* 1-3, 12-15. Ithaca, NY: RCCP, Cornell University.

Gibson, J. (2005). Reflections on a conference workshop. *Refocus, 11,* 1-3, 7-10. Ithaca, NY: RCCP, Cornell University.

Goleman, D. (1995). *Emotional intelligence.* New York: Bantam.

Goleman, D. (1998). *Working with emotional intelligence.* New York: Bantam.

Greene, R. (2001). *The explosive child.* New York: Harper Collins Publishers, Inc.

Greene, R., & Ablon, J. (2006). *Treating explosive kids: The collaborative problem-solving approach.* New York: The Guilford Press.

Greenspan, S. (1999). *Building healthy minds.* New York: Da Capo Press.

Group Child Care Consultants. (1977). *Basic course for residential child care workers.* Chapel Hill, NC: Group Child Care Consultant Services.

Hansell, N. (1976). *The person-in-distress: On the biosocial dynamics of adaptation.* New York: Human Sciences Press.

Hardy, K., & Laszloffy, T. (2005). *Teens who hurt.* New York: Guilford Press.

Harris, J. R. (1998). *The nurture assumption: Why children turn out the way they do.* New York: Free Press.

Harris, J. R. (2006). Are peers more important than parents during the process of development? Yes (reprint of Wilson Quarterly article). In A. M. Guest (Ed.), *Taking sides: Clashing views in lifespan development.* Dubuque, Iowa: McGraw-Hill/Dushkin.

Hawkins-Rodgers, Y. (2007). Adolescents adjusting to a group home environment: A residential care model of re-organizing attachment behavior and building resiliency. *Children and Youth Services Review, 29,* 1121-1141.

Hobbs, N. (1975). *The futures of children.* San Francisco: Jossey-Bass.

Holden, M. J. (1983). *Team development.* Columbus, OH: Ohio Association of Child Care Workers, Inc.

Holden, M. J., & Holden, J. C. (1990). Learning life skills. *Journal of Child and Youth Care Work, 6,* 45-54.

Holden, M. J., & the TCI Instructors of the RCCP (2009). *Therapeutic crisis intervention, reference guide. (6th ed.).* Ithaca, NY: Cornell University.

Holmqvist, R., Hill, T., & Lang, A. (2007). Treatment alliance in residential treatment of criminal adolescents. *Child Youth Care Forum, 36,* 163-178.

Howe, D., Brandon, M., Hinings, D., & Schofield, G. (1999). *Attachment theory, child maltreatment and family support: A practice and assessment model.* New Jersey: Lawrence Erlbaum Associates.

Howes, C. (1999). Attachment relationships in the context of multiple caregivers. In J. Cassidy, & P.R. Shaver (Eds.), *Handbook of attachment: Theory, research, and clinical applications* (pp. 671-687). New York: Guilford Press.

Hubble, M., Duncan, B., & Miller, S. (1999). *The heart & soul of change: What works in therapy.* Washington, D.C.: American Psychological Association.

Hutchins, D.E., & Vaught, C.C. (1997). *Helping relationships and strategies* (3rd ed.). Pacific Grove, CA: Brooks/Cole.

Ivey, A., & Ivey, M. (2003). *Intentional interviewing and counseling: Facilitating client development in a multicultural society.* Pacific Grove, CA: Brooks/Cole-Thomson Learning.

Johnson, D., & Johnson, F. (1975). *Joining together: Group theory and group skills.* Upper Saddle River, NJ: Prentice-Hall, Inc.

Jones, K. (Ed.). (2001). *Readings in human behavior.* Mason, OH:

Thomson Learning Custom Publishing.

Kohn, A. (1999). *Punished by rewards: The trouble with gold stars, incentive plans, A's, praise and other bribes (2nd ed.)*. Boston: Houghton Mifflin.

Krueger, M. (1983). *Intervention techniques for child/youth care workers*. Milwaukee, WI: TALL Publishing.

Krueger, M. (1994). Rhythm and presence: Connecting with children on the edge. *Journal of Emotional and Behavioral Problems, 3*(1), 49-51.

Krueger, M. (2007). Four areas of support for child and youth care workers. *Families in Society, 88*(2), 233-240.

Krueger, M., Glaovits, L., Wilder, Q., & Pick, M. (1999). *A curriculum guide for working with youth: An interactive approach*. Milwaukee, WI: University Outreach Press.

Lambert, M. (1992). Implications for outcome research for psychotherapy integration. In J. C. Norcross & M. R Goldstein (Eds.), *Handbook of psychotherapy integration* (pp. 94-129). New York: Basic Books.

Lanyado, M. (2001). Daring to try again: The hope and pain of forming new attachments. *Therapeutic Communities, 22*(1).

Laursen, E., & Birmingham, S. (2003). Caring relationships as a protective factor for at-risk youth: An ethnographic study. *Families in Society: The Journal of Contemporary Human Services, 84*(2), 240-246.

Lieberman, A. F., & Knorr, K. K. (2007). The impact of trauma: A developmental framework for infancy and early childhood. *Psychiatric Annals, 37*(6), 416-422.

Long, N. (1995). Why adults strike back: Learned behavior or genetic code? *Reclaiming children & youth, 4*(1), 11-15.

Lovett, H. (1996). *Learning to listen: Positive approaches and people with difficult behaviour*. Baltimore, MD: Paul H. Brooks Publishing Co.

Maier, H. (1982). To be attached and free. The challenge of child development. *Child Welfare, 61*(2), 67-76.

Maier, H. (1987). *Developmental group care of children and youth.* New York: Haworth Press, Inc.

Maier, H. (1991). Developmental foundations of youth care work. In J. Beker & Z. Eisikovits (Eds.), *Knowledge utilization in residential child and youth care practice* (pp. 25-48). Washington, DC: Child Welfare League of America.

Maier, H. (1991). An exploration of the substance of child and youth care practice. *Child and Youth Care Forum, 20*(6), 393-411.

Maier, H. (1992). Rhythmicity—a powerful force for experiencing unity and personal connections. *Journal of Child and Youth Care Work, 5,* 7-13.

Maier, H. (1994). Attachment development is "in." *Journal of Child and Youth Care, 9*(1), 35-51.

Malekoff, A. (1997). *Group work with adolescents: Principles and practice (Social work practice with children and families).* London: Guilford.

Maluccio, A. (1991). Interpersonal and group life in residential care: A competence-centered, ecological perspective. In J. Beker & Z. Eisikovits (Eds.). *Knowledge utilization in residential child and youth care practice* (pp. 49-63). Washington, DC: Child Welfare League of America.

Maluccio, A., & Sinanoglu, P. (1981). *The challenge of partnership: Working with parents of children in foster care.* Washington, DC: Child Welfare League of America.

Maslow, A. (1969). *Toward a psychology of being (2nd ed.).* New York: D. Van Nostrand.

Maslow, A. (1987). *Motivation and personality (3rd ed.).* New York: Harper Row.

Masten, A. (2001). Ordinary magic: Resilience processes in development. *American Psychologist, 56,* 227-238.

Masten, A. (2004). Regulatory processes, risk, and resilience in adolescent development. *Annals of the New York Academy of Sciences, 1021,* 310–319.

Masten, A., & Coatsworth, D. (1998). The development of competence in favorable and unfavorable environments. *American Psychologist, 53*(2),105-220.

Masten, A., & Reed, M. (2002). Resilience in development. In C. Snyder & S. Copey (Eds.), *Handbook of Positive Psychology* (pp. 74-88). New York: Oxford University Press.

Mayer, M. (1978). *A guide for child-care workers.* New York: The Child Welfare League of America.

Mohr, W. K., Martin, A., Olson, J. N., Pumariega, A. J., & Branca, N. (2009). Beyond point and level systems: Moving toward child-centered programming. *American Journal of Orthopsychiatry, 79*(1), 8-18.

Montessori, M. (1912). *The Montessori method: Scientific pedagogy as applied to child education in "the children's houses."* New York: Frederick A. Stokes Company.

Moses, T. (2000). Attachment theory and residential treatment: A study of staff-client relationships. *American Journal of Orthopsychiatry, 70*(4), 474-490.

Nelson, C. (2002). Neural development and life-long plasticity. In R. Lerner, F. Jacobs, D. Wetlieb (Eds.), *Promoting positive child, adolescent, and family development: Handbook of program and policy interventions* (pp. 31-60). Thousand Oaks, CA: Sage Publications.

Nelson, J. (1996). *Positive discipline.* New York: Ballantine Books.

Owusu-Bempah, J., & Howitt, D. (1997). Socio-genealogical connectedness, attachment theory, and childcare practice. *Child and Family Social Work Practice, 2*, 199-207.

Owusu-Bempah, J., & Howitt, D. (2002). Addressing cultural diversity, addressing racism. *The Psychologist, 15*(6), 293-295.

Pajares, F., & Urdan, T. (eds) (2006). *Self-efficacy beliefs of adolescents.* Greenwich, CT: Information Age Publishing.

Pasztor, E., Polowy, M., Wasson, D., & Wolf, M. (1987). *Preparing youth for interdependent living.* Atlanta, GA: Child Welfare Institute and University of Connecticut.

Perry, B. (1997). Incubated in terror: Neurodevelopmental factors in the 'cycle of violence.' In J. Osofsky (Ed.), *Children, youth and violence: The search for solutions.* New York: Guildford Press.

Perry, B. (2002a). *Helping traumatized children: A brief overview for care givers.* Available online at www.ChildTrauma.org. The Child Trauma Academy.

Perry, B. (2002b). *Stress, trauma and post-traumatic stress disorders in children.* Available online at www.ChildTrauma.org. The Child Trauma Academy.

Perry, B. ,& Pollard, R. (1998). Homeostasis, stress, trauma and adaptation: A neurodevelopmental view of childhood trauma. *Child and Adolescent Psychiatric Clinics of North America, 7,* 33-51.

Piaget, J. (1951). *Play, dreams and imitation in childhood.* London: Heineman.

Prothrow-Stith, D. & Weissman, M. (1993). *Deadly consequences.* Canada: Harper Collins Publishers, Inc.

Redl, F., & Wineman, D. (1952). *Controls from within; Techniques for the treatment of the aggressive child.* New York: The Free Press.

Reiter, S., & Bryen, D. (1991). Promoting social competence: Implications of work with mentally retarded children and adults in residential settings. In J. Beker & Z. Eisikovits (Eds.), *Knowledge utilization in residential child and youth care practice* (pp. 25-48). Washington, DC: Child Welfare League of America.

Robins, J. (1987). *The lost children of Ireland: A study of charity children in Ireland 1700-1900.* Dublin: Institute of Public Administration.

Rosen, M. (1999). Treating child welfare children in residential settings. *Children & Youth Services Review, 21*, 657-676.

Ruch, G. (2005). Relationship-based practice and reflective practice: Holistic approaches to contemporary child care social work. *Child and Family Social Work, 10*, 111-123.

Ruch, G. (2007). Reflective practice in contemporary child-care social work: The role of containment. *British Journal of Social Work, 37*, 659-680.

Salovey, P., Mayer, J., & Caruso, D. (2002). The positive psychology of emotional intelligence. In C. R. Snyder & S. J. Lopez (Eds.), *The handbook of positive psychology* (pp. 159-171). New York: Oxford University Press.

Schein, E. (2004). *Organizational culture and leadership, (3rd ed.).* New York: Wiley Publisher.

Schofield, G., & Beek, M. (2005). Providing a secure base: Parenting children in long-term foster family care. *Attachment & Human Development, 7*(1), 3-25.

Schon, D. (1996). *The reflective practitioner: How professionals think in action.* New York: Basic Books, Inc.

Schore, A. (2001). The effects of relational trauma on right brain development, affect regulation, and infant mental health. *Infant Mental Health Journal, 22*, 7-66.

Shiendling, S. (1995). The therapeutic diamond: A model for effective staff communication and intervention in residential treatment settings for children who are emotionally disturbed. *Residential Treatment for Children & Youth, 12*(3), 45-55.

Siegel, D. (1999). *The developing mind: Toward a neurobiology of interpersonal experience.* New York: Guilford.

Stewart, J. (2002). *Beyond time out: A practical guide to understanding and serving students with behavioral impairments in the public schools.* Gorham, ME: Hastings Clinical

Associates.

Swick, K. J. (2007). Empower foster parents toward caring relations with children. *Early Childhood Education Journal, 34*(6), 393-398.

Trieschman, A., Whittaker, J., & Brendtro, L. (1969). *The other 23 hours: Child care work with emotionally disturbed children in a therapeutic milieu.* Chicago: Aldine.

United States General Accounting Office. (1994). *Residential care: Some high-risk youth benefit, but more study needed.* (Available from GAO, P.O. Box 6015, Gaithersburg, No 20884-6015).

van der Kolk, B. A. (2005). Developmental trauma disorder: Towards a rational diagnosis for children with complex trauma histories. *Psychiatric Annals, 33*(5), 401-408.

van der Kolk, B., & Ducey, C. (1989). The psychological processing of traumatic experience: Rorschach patterns in PTSD. *Journal of Traumatic Stress, 2*(2), 59-274.

VanderVen, K. (1999). You are what you do and become what you've done: The role of activity in development of self. *Journal of Child and Youth Care, 13*(2), 133-147.

VanderVen, K. (2000). Cultural aspects of point and level systems. *Reclaiming Children and Youth, 9*(1), 53-59.

VanderVen, K. (2005). Beyond game boys, Walkmans, and TV: The significance of activities and activity programming in group and residential care. *Residential Group Care Quarterly, 5*(3), 12-16.

Vorrath, H., & Brendtro, L. (1985). *Positive peer culture (2nd ed.).* New York: Aldine Publishing Company.

Vygotsky, L. (1978). *Mind and society: The development of higher mental processes.* Cambridge, MA: Harvard University Press.

Ward, A. (2004). Towards a theory of the everyday: The ordinary and the special in daily living in residential care. *Child and*

Youth Care Forum, 33(3), 209-225.

Watson, J. (1896). Reformatory and industrial schools. *Journal of the Royal Statistical Society, 59*(2), 255-317.

Weiner, A. (1991). Providing a development-enhancing environment: The child and youth care worker as observer and interpreter of behavior. In J. Beker & Z. Eisikovits (Eds.), *Knowledge utilization in residential child and youth care practice* (pp. 25-48). Washington, DC: Child Welfare League of America.

Weiner, A., & Weiner, E. (1990). *Expanding the options in child placement.* Lanham, MD: University Press of America.

Wells-Wilbon, R., & McDowell, E. (2001). Cultural competence and sensitivity: Getting it right. Cultural and societal influences. *Child and Adolescent Psychiatry, 10*(4), 679-693.

Werner, E. (1990). Protective factors and individual resilience. In S. Meisels and J. Shonkoff (Eds.), *Handbook of early childhood intervention.* Cambridge, England: Cambridge University Press.

Whittaker, J., & Pfeiffer, S. (1994). Research priorities for residential group child care. *Child Welfare, 73*, 583-601.

Wolfensberger, W. (1972). *The principle of normalization in human services.* Toronto: National Institute on Mental Retardation.

Wolins, M. (1967). *Selected works of Janusz Korczak.* Springfield, VA: U.S. Department of Commerce.

Zegers, M. A. M., Schuengel, C., Van IJzendoorn, M. H., & Janssens, J. (2008). Attachment and problem behavior of adolescents during residential treatment. *Attachment & Human Development, 10*(1), 91-103.

Zielinski, D., & Bradshaw, C. (2006). Ecological influences on the sequelae of child maltreatment: A review of the literature. *Child Maltreatment, 11*(1), 49-62.

Additional Resources

Adler, J. (1981). *Fundamentals of group care*. Massachusetts: Ballinger Publishing Company.

Ainsworth, F., & Fulcher, L. (1981). *Group care for children*. London: Tavistock Publications.

Anglin, J. P., & Working Group. (1978). Residential child care programming: Standards and guidelines; Chapter VI. In *Children's residential care facilities: Proposed standards and guidelines*. Toronto: Children's Services Division, Ministry of Community and Social Services.

Arieli, M. (1997). *The occupational experience of residential child and youth care workers: Caring and its discontents*. Binghamton, NY: Haworth Press, Inc.

Association for Child and Youth Care Practice. (2001). *Competencies for professional child and youth work personnel*. North American Certification Project. [Electronic version] available online at www.acycp.org.

Beek, M. (1999). Parenting children with attachment difficulties. *Adoption & Fostering, 23*(1), 16-23.

Beker, J., & Eisikovits, Z. (Eds.). (1991). *Knowledge utilization in residential child and youth care practice*. Washington, DC: Child Welfare League of America.

Benson, J. F. (2005). *Working more creatively with groups (2nd ed.)*. Oxford: Routledge.

Berlin, I. (1997). Attachment theory: Its use in milieu therapy and in psychotherapy with children in residential treatment. *Residential Treatment for Children & Youth, 15*(2), 29-37.

Bloom, S. (2005). The sanctuary model of organizational change for children's residential treatment. *Therapeutic Community: The International Journal for Therapeutic and Supportive Organizations, 26*(1), 65-81.

Boylan, J., & Ing, I. (2005). "Seen but not heard"—young people's experience of advocacy. *International Journal of Social Welfare, 12*, 2-12.

Brookfield, S. (1987). *Developing critical thinkers.* San Francisco: Jossey-Bass.

Brown, A., & Clough, R. (Eds.). (1989). *Groups and groupings; Life and work in day and residential settings.* London and New York: Tavistock/Routledge.

Brown, E., Bullock, R., Hobson, C., & Little, M. (1998). *Making residential child care work: Structure and culture in children's homes.* Brookfield, VT: Adgate.

Chowdhury, S., Endres, M., & Lanis, T. (2002). Preparing students for success in team work environments: The importance of building confidence. *Journal of Managerial Issues, 14*(3), 346-359.

Code of ethics: Standards of practice of North American child & youth care professionals. (1995). The Association for Child & Youth Care Practice, Inc. Available online at www.acycp.org/code of.htm.

Coles, R. (1990). *The spiritual life of children.* Boston: Houghton Miflin.

Conyne, R. (1999). *Failures in group work—How we can learn from our mistakes.* California: Sage Publications, Inc.

Daniels, M. (1982). The development of the concept of self-actualization in the writings of Abraham Maslow. *Current Psychological Reviews, 2*, 61-76.

De Civita, M., & Dobkin, P. (2004). Pediatric adherence as a multidimensional and dynamic construct, involving a triadic partnership. *Journal of Pediatric Psychology, 29*(3), 157-169.

Department of Health and Human Services. (2005). *Roadmap to seclusion and restraint free mental health services* (Publication No. (SMA) 05-4055). Rockville, MD: Center for Mental Health Services, Substance Abuse and Mental Health Services Administration.

Douglas, T. (1986). *Group living; The application of group dynamics in residential settings.* New York: Tavistock Publications.

Durrant, M. (1993). *Residential treatment: A cooperative, competency-cased approach to therapy and program design.* New York: W. W. Norton & Company.

Ettin, M., Cohen, B., & Fidler, J. (1997). Group-as-a-whole theory viewed in its 20th-century context. *Group Dynamics, 1*(4), 329-340.

Fewster, G. (1990a). Growing together: The personal relationship in child and youth care work. *Perspectives In Professional Child And Youth Care, 13*(1), 25-40.

Fluegelman, A. (1974). *The new games book.* New York: Doubleday.

Forsyth, D. R. (1983). *An introduction to group dynamics.* Pacific Grove: Brooks/Cole.

Freud, A., & Burlingham, D. ([1944]1973). Infants without families: The case for and against residential nurseries. In A. Freud, *The writings of Anna Freud: Vol. 3* (pp. 1939-1945). New York: International Universities Press, 543-664.

Friedman, M. (2000). *Post traumatic stress disorder: The latest assessment and treatment strategies.* Kansas City, MO: Compact Clinical.

Frost, N., Mills, S., & Stein, M. (1999). *Understanding residential child care.* London: Ashgate Publishing Limited.

Gagne, R. (1985). *The conditions of learning and the theory of instruction.* Fort Worth, TX: Holt, Rinehart, and Winston, Inc.

Gagne, R., Briggs, L., & Wager, W. (1992). *Principles of instructional design.* Forth Worth, TX: Harcourt Brace College Publishers.

Gagne, R., & Medsker, K. (1996). *The conditions of learning: Training applications.* Fort Worth, TX: Harcourt Brace College Publishers.

Gibson, J., Leonard, M., & Wilson, M. (2004). Changing residential child care: A systems approach to consultation training and development. *Child Care in Practice, 10*(4), 345-357.

Glisson, C., Dukes, D., & Green, P. (2006). The effects of the ARC organizational intervention on caseworker turnover, climate and culture in children's service systems. *Child Abuse & Neglect: An International Journal, 30*(8), 855-880.

Glisson, C., & Hemmelgarn, A. (1998). The effects of organizational climate and interorganizational coordination on the quality and outcomes of children's service systems. *Child Abuse & Neglect: An International Journal, 22*(5), 401-421.

Goffman, E. (1968). *Asylums: Essays on the social situation of mental patients and other inmates.* Harmondsworth: Penguin.

Goldstein, A. (1999). *The prepare curriculum: Teaching prosocial competencies.* Champaign, IL: Research Press.

Gordon, C. (1999). A parenting programme for parents of children with disturbed attachment patterns. *Adoption & Fostering, 23*(4),49-56.

Greenspan, S., & Wieder, S. (1998). *The child with special needs: Encouraging intellectual and emotional growth.* New York: Da Capo Press.

Grover, S. (2004). Advocating for children's rights as an aspect of professionalism: The role of frontline workers and children's rights commissions. *Child & Youth Care Forum, 3*(6), 405-423.

Gulley, H. (1968). *Discussion, conference and group process.* New York: Holt, Rinehart and Winston, Inc.

Hanley, S., & Abell, S. (2002). Maslow and relatedness: Creating an interpersonal model of self-actualization. *Journal of Humanistic Psychology, 42*(4), 37-57.

Hanson, R., & Spratt, E. (2000). Reactive attachment disorder: What we know about the disorder and implications for treatment. *Child Maltreatment, 5*(2), 137-145.

Hartsell, J. (2008). *Sisyphus and the itsy-bitsy spider: Working with children.* Dryden, NY: Ithaca Press.

Herman, J. (1997). *Trauma and recovery.* New York: Basic Books.

Heron, G., & Chakrabarti, M. (2003). Exploring the perceptions of staff towards children and young people living in community-based children's homes. *Journal of Social Work, 3*(1), 81-98.

Holden, J. C. (2009). *Developing competent crisis intervention trainers: Assessing the disparity of participant's curriculum knowledge/skills and training skills in a crisis intervention train-the-trainer program.* Köln, Germany: Lambert Academic Publishing.

Holden, M. J. (1986). *The group.* Columbus, OH: Ohio Association of Child Care Workers, Inc.

Homans, G. C. (1968). *The human group.* London: Unwin Brothers Limited.

Howes, C., Shivers, E., & Ritchie, S. (2004). Improving social relationships in child care through a researcher-program partnership. *Early Education & Development, 15*(1).

Huitt, W. (2004). *Maslow's hierarchy of needs.* Educational Psychology Interactive, Valdosta, GA: Valdosta State University.

Jones, M. (1978). *Maturation of the therapeutic community: An organic approach to health and mental health.* New York: Human Sciences Press.

Kerr T., & Straughan, P. (1988). *T.E.A.M. challenge; Facilitator training manual (4th ed.).* Ithaca, NY: Cayuga Nature Center.

Kiraly, M. (2001). *Residential child care staff selection: Choose with care.* Binghamton, NY: Haworth Press, Inc.

Knopka, G. (1972). *Social group work: A helping process.* Englewood Cliffs, NJ: Prentice Hall Inc.

Ko, S. J., Ford, J. D., Kassam-Adams, N., Berkowitz, S. J., Wilson, C., Wong, M., Brymer, M. J., & Layne, C. M. (2008). Creating trauma-informed systems: Child welfare, education, first responders, health care, juvenile justice. *Professional Psychology: Research and Practice, 39*(4), 396-404.

LaVigna, G., & Donnellan, A. (1997). *Alternatives to punishment.* New York: Irvington Publishers, Inc.

Lawson, L. (1998). Milieu management of traumatized youngsters. *Journal of Child and Adolescent Psychiatric Nursing,11*(3), 99-114.

Ledoux, J. (2002). *Synaptic self: How our brains become who we are.* New York: Viking.

Legends & Legacies (1999). Available online at www.legends.ca/orphanages/orphanHistory.html

Levi, D. (2001). *Group dynamics for teams.* London: Sage Publications.

Lewin, K. (1936). *Principles of topological psychology.* New York: McGraw-Hill.

Luft, J. (1984). *Group process: An introduction to group dynamics.* San Francisco: Mayfield Publishing Company.

Maier, H. (1961). *Group living: A unique feature in residential treatment (New perspectives on services to groups: Theory, organization and practice).* New York: National Association of Social Workers.

Moore, K., Moretti, M., & Holland, R. (1998). A new perspective on youth care programs: Using attachment theory to guide interventions for troubled youth. *Residential Treatment for Children & Youth, 15*(3), 1-24.

Nelson, C. (2000). The neurobiological bases of early intervention. In J. P. Shonkoff & S. J. Meisels (Eds.), *Handbook of early childhood intervention, second edition* (pp. 204-227). Cambridge, MA: Cambridge University Press.

Nelson, C., Bloom, F., Cameron, J., Amaral, D., Dahl, R., & Pine, D. (2002). An integrative multidisciplinary approach to the study of brain-behavior relations in the context of typical and atypical development. *Developmental Psychopathology: Special issue on multiple levels of analysis, 14,* 499-520.

Nelson, C., & Parker, S. (2005). The impact of early institutional rearing on the ability to discriminate facial expressions of emotion: An event-related potential study. *Child Development, 76*(1), 54-72.

North American Association for Child and Youth Care Practice. (2001). *Competencies for professional child and youth work personnel: The North American certification project.*

Packard, T. (2001). Enhancing staff commitment through organizational values: The case of a homeless shelter. *Administration in Social Work, 2593,* 35-52.

Parker, R. (1988). *Residential care for children in residential care: The research reviewed (Ed. I. Sinclair).* London: Her Majesty's Stationery Office.

Parry, P. (1995). One lesson that didn't lessen, or the power of five simple actions. *Journal of Child and Youth Care, 10*(2), 43-48.

Payne, M. (2005). *The origins of social work. Continuity and change.* New York: Palgrave MacMillan.

Polsky, W. (1962). *Cottage six: The social system of delinquent boys in residential treatment.* New York: John Wiley.

Prochaska, J., DiClemente, C., & Norcross, J. (1992). In search of how people change: Applications to addictive behaviors. *American Psychologist, 47*(9) 1102-1114.

Quality Assurance Agency for Higher Education. (2000). *Social policy and administration, and social work.* Gloucester, UK: Quality Assurance Agency for Higher Education.

Richardson, B. (2001). *Working with challenging youth.* Philadelphia: Brunner-Routledge Taylor & Francis Group.

Ringer, T. (2002). *Group action: The dynamics of groups in therapeutic, educational and corporate settings.* London: Jessica Kingsley Publishers.

Rivard, J., Bloom, S., Abramovitz, R., Pasquale, L., Duncan, M., McCorkle, D., et al. (2003). Assessing the implementation and effects of a trauma-focused intervention for youths in residential treatment. *Psychiatric Quarterly, 74*(2), 137-154.

Rose, L. (1990). On being a child and youth care worker. *Journal of Child And Youth Care, 5*(1), 21-26.

Rose, M. (1988). The function of food in a residential treatment process. *Residential Treatment for Children & Youth, 6*(1), 43-61.

Sanborn, J. (1994). *Bag of tricks II.* Florissant, CO: Search Publications.

Schiff, M., Nebe, S., & Gilman, R. (2006). Life satisfaction among Israeli youth in residential treatment care. *British Journal of Social Work, 36,* 1325-1343.

Schwartz, T., & Schultz, B. (1992). Teamwork as a function of treatment. *Residential Treatment of Children & Youth, 9*(2), 49-53.

Scott, D. (2003). Spirituality in child and youth care: Considering spiritual development and "relational consciousness". *Child and Youth Care Forum, 32*(2), 117-131.

Scottish Social Services Council. (2004). *Occupational competencies for residential care personnel.* Glasgow.

Simon, S., Howe, L., & Kirschenbaum, H. (1972). *Values clarification: A handbook of practical strategies for teachers and students.* New York: Hart Publishing Company, Inc.

Stormont, M., Lewis, T., & Smith, S. (2005). Behavior support strategies in early childhood settings. *Journal of Positive Behavior Interventions, 7*(3), 131-139.

Swaffer, T., & Hollin, C. (1997). Adolescents' experiences of anger in a residential setting. *Journal of Adolescence, 20,* 567-575.

Terr, L. (1990). *Too scared to cry: Psychic trauma in childhood.* New York: Harper and Row.

The National Resource Center for Youth Services. (1986). *University of Oklahoma advanced training course for residential child care workers.* Oklahoma: The Oklahoma Board of Regents.

Thomas, S., Shattell, M., & Martin, T. (2002). What's therapeutic about the therapeutic milieu? *Archives of Psychiatric Nursing, XVI*(3), 99-107.

Trelfa, J. (2005). Faith in reflective practice. *Reflective Practice,* 6(2), 205-212.

Tuckman, B., & Jensen, M. (1977). Stages of small group development. *Journal of Group and Organisational Studies, 24.*

United Kingdom Quality Assurance Agency for Higher Education. (2000). *Social policy and administration and social work.* Glouester, UK: Quality Assurance Agency for Higher Education.

van der Kolk, B. A. (1994). Childhood abuse and neglect and loss of self-regulation. *Bulletin of the Menninger Clinic, 58,* 145-168.

VanderVen, K. (1998). Views from the field: Something old and a vision. *Journal of Child and Youth Care, 12*(3), 87-90.

VanderVen, K., & Tittnich, E. (1985). *Competent caregivers—competent children.* New York: The Hawthorne Press.

Vander Zanden, J. (2000). *Human development, (7th ed.).* Boston: McGraw-Hill Higher Education.

Ward, A. (1993). *Working in group care—social work in residential and day care settings.* Birmingham, UK: Venture Press.

Webb, N., (Ed.). (2006). *Working with traumatized youth in child welfare.* New York: The Guilford Press.

Whittaker, J. (2000). Reinventing residential childcare: an agenda for research and practice. *Family-centered Services In Residential Treatment, 17*(3), 13-30.

Whittaker, J., & Trieschman, A., (Eds.). (1972). *Children away from home: A sourcebook of residential treatment.* Chicago: Aldine.

Wills, D. (1960). *Throw away thy rod: Living with difficult children.* London: Victor Gollancz Ltd.

Wills, D. (1970). *A place like home. A pioneer hostel for boys.* London: George Allen and Unwin Ltd.

Wills, D. (1971). *Spare the child.* Harmondsworth, Middlesex, England: Penguin Education Specials, Penguin.

Wilson, L. (1989). *Brehon Laws.* Available online at www.irishsociety.org/Hedgemaster%20Archives/brehon_laws.htm.

Winnicott, C. (1971). *Child care and social work.* London: Bookstall Services.

Working with aggressive youth: A sourcebook for child-care providers. (1989). Omaha, NE: Father Flanagan's Boys' Home.

Youll, P., & McCourt-Perring, C. (1993). *Raising voices: Ensuring quality in residential care.* London: HMSO.

Zastrow, C. (1997). *Social work with groups.* Chicago: Nelson-Hall Publishers.

Zimmerman, D. (2002). Research and practice in social and life skills training. *Residential Treatment for Children & Youth, 20*(2), 51-75.

Zimmerman, D., & Cohler, B. (2000). From disciplinary control to benign milieu in children's residential treatment. *Residential Treatment for Children & Youth, 18*(2), 27-54.

INDEX

R

S